The Handbook

OF

Program Management

How to Facilitate Project Success with Optimal Program Management

JAMES T. BROWN

New York   Chicago   San Francisco   Lisbon   London   Madrid   Mexico City
Milan   New Delhi   San Juan   Seoul   Singapore   Sydney   Toronto

The *McGraw·Hill* Companies

1 2 3 4 5 6 7 8 9 0 FGR/FGR 0 9 8 7

ISBN 13: 978-0-07-149472-4
ISBN 10:0-07-149472-3

This publication is designed to provide accurate and authoritative information in regard to the subject matter covered. It is sold with the understanding that the publisher is not engaged in rendering legal, accounting, or other professional service. If legal advice or other expert assistance is required, the services of a competent professional person should be sought.

> ——*From a Declaration of Principles jointly adopted by a Committee of the American Bar Association and a Committee of Publishers and Associations*

McGraw-Hill books are available at special quantity discounts to use as premiums and sales promotions, or for use in corporate training programs. For more information, please write to the Director of Special Sales, Professional Publishing, McGraw-Hill, Two Penn Plaza, New York, NY 10121-2298. Or contact your local bookstore.

This book is printed on acid-free paper.

Library of Congress Cataloging-in-Publication Data

Brown, James T.
  The handbook of program management : how to facilitate project success with optimal program management / James T. Brown.
     p. cm.
  Includes index.
  ISBN-13: 978-0-07-149472-4 (hardcover : alk. paper)
  ISBN-10: 0-07-149472-3
  1. Project management—Handbooks, manuals, etc. I. Title.
HD69.P75B762 2007
658.4'04—dc22   2007013901

*This book is dedicated to the memory of my father,
L. J. Brown, a Marine's Marine who taught me
the value of discipline and hard work.*

Acknowledgments

To all those who took time out of their busy schedules to provide valuable feedback on this book; to the thousands of participants in my training classes who I have listened to and learned from over the years; and to my clients, former NASA colleagues and leadership—it has indeed been my pleasure to work with you.

I would be remiss without pointing out the names of some key individuals who either contributed directly or indirectly to this work or my personal development. In alphabetical order: Dr. Robert Armacost, Timothy Bollo, Janice S. Brown, Judith Elaine Brown, Vanessa F. Brown, Chuck Bucher, Dwayne Burns, Terry Clark, Dawn Crooks, Hugo Delgado, Valerie Denson, Ron Dittemore, Deborah Gaines, Sandy Geroux, Lyndon Godwin, Carl Green, Labiche Ferreira, William R. Humphries, James L. Jennings, Dawn Josephson, Stacy Kirpatrick, Michael C. Kostelnik, Dick Lyon, Howard Miller, Alison Mills Long, George Morrisey, Arlene McClurg, Charlie Murphy, Jessica Pelham, Tim Pelham, Dennis Peters, Amy Piper, Stephen Pittotti, Bob Rich, Joyce Rozewski, Marilyn Scott, Ralf Schulman, Roland Seidl, Tip Talone, John Washek, Sandeep Wilkhu, Rick Williams, and Ben Wilson.

Ben Wilson and Stacy Kirpatrick went the extra mile in the review process and I am especially appreciative for their efforts.

I am very grateful to my wife Vanessa, and my sons Jonathan and Steven for enduring the long hours and juggled family schedule that was necessary to make this book a reality.

Contents

Introduction

The advantage—the competitive-edge, leading companies today seek—is process. Why is process important to a company and to program management? Just look at the nightly news. A month or a quarter doesn't go by without some widely recognized organization or company publicly acknowledging a major project disappointment. Additionally, the late-delivery and cost overruns of projects often cause turmoil and upheaval within organizations. That's why the companies that survive and thrive today and that will survive the future will be those that have processes in place and can repeatedly integrate new people and new technology into their existing processes, thus producing superior products and services.

While technology and people are definitely important, they are just inputs that support the process. Process allows an organization to exist ten years from now when most of the technology is different from today's and a good portion of the workforce has changed.

For example, examine the products Dell made and sold ten years ago versus what they make and sell today. Dell has a process that allows them to take relatively new technology and people to produce a quality product. What those products will be ten years from now is anyone's guess, but Dell has processes in place that will facilitate their development. Yes, innovation can still be a driving force for a company, but innovation without process is short-lived. In fact, companies with a pure innovation strategy usually have a process for that.

This leads us to the role of the program manager—the individual who is responsible for delivering a major product or service, while improving that product or service and enabling the organization to continually outperform the competition. This book is for that individual.

In the following chapters we will focus on the processes that make a program manager successful at incorporating new technology and new people while delivering improved products and services that continually outpace the competition. Many books already address project management and operations management. That's why this book addresses program management at the point where operations and project management collide, as that's precisely when the program manager must maintain a culture of repeatable success.

The operations environment without change is very stable. However, we all know that change in any business is inevitable. Change makes its way to the operations environment through the implementation of projects. Therefore, the focus of this book is the establishment of a project management culture that allows for successful completion of projects in the dynamic program environment.

This book provides a framework of structured, organized common sense. Successful program management is not magical, complicated, or difficult. However, it requires leadership and integrity to repeatedly execute successfully. You can accomplish this with sophisticated software packages and cadres of consultants. Or you can accomplish this with a calendar and a notebook. Numerous organizations have attempted to buy their way to a successful project management culture by purchasing tools or hiring consultants, only to fail because of a lack of leadership and integrity to follow structured, organized common sense. Tools and consultants in the absence of structured, organized common sense usually result in program and project failures that have pretty charts and diagrams to communicate why they are over budget and behind schedule.

Strong leadership at the business and program level results in repeatable success. Exceptional project managers may be able to deliver success in isolation or sporadically in the absence of leadership, but even the best project managers fail on occasion when they work in environments that lack leadership. More often than not, project failure is not the project manager's fault, although he or she is frequently blamed. The real cause for the failure is faulty program management.

If you believe that project management is not complicated and the majority of professionals today can be effective project managers when provided an environment that facilitates their development and success, then this book is for you. Realize that you won't find complex methodologies or "whiz-bang" quick fixes here; rather, the principles provided in this book will assist you in establishing a successful project management culture where the program acts with integrity and supporting personnel and stakeholders are not apathetic but fully engaged and supportive. You can employ some of these principles right now with immediate results, while others may require a longer-term implementation strategy. Either way, you'll have the tools and information you need to strengthen your program management processes so you can have repeated project management success.

Finally, to the reader, Oliver Wendell Holmes, Jr., stated "A moment's insight is sometimes worth a lifetime's experience." It is my hope that this book provides you many insightful tips and practices that provide a positive, lasting impact on you and your organization.

If you have a comment on this book or how your experiences relate to something in it, I would enjoy hearing from you. Please contact me at james@sebasolutions.com.

Chaos to Clarity

The organization that can learn, change, adapt, and do so rapidly is destined for success. Unfortunately, many of today's organizations exist in a state of chaos, meaning that learning, changing, and adapting are not the norm. These companies exist in this dysfunctional state because they do not have an effective program management structure in place. And without great program management, no business can readily adapt to changing business conditions. However, truly great program managers turn this chaos into clarity by creating a culture that facilitates success.

Program and Project Management Roles

The role of the program manager is very different from the role of the project manager. The role of the program manager is very complex; it can vary from managing multiple projects to managing multiple projects with operational responsibilities, in addition to being accountable for profit or cost targets linked to business strategy. Conversely, the project manager's role is to deliver the project within the cost and schedule constraints that are usually established at the program level.

The program manager is also frequently accountable for the "policy" that defines how the work is accomplished. Even in environments where a Project Management Office (PMO) establishes company- or organization-wide policy with regard to project management, the program manager often plays a significant role, since this policy directly impacts his or her ability to meet cost targets and business objectives.

In addition to making sure the company meets program objectives, the program manager must establish a culture that allows his or her project managers to be successful. The program manager must create, manage, and continually improve the culture that enables successful projects.

A program manager is first and foremost a leader. In fact, the program manager's main leadership duty is to turn chaos into clarity for the team. Any leader who allows chaos to exist or just passes chaos down to the team without clarification is not exercising leadership. People need clear direction and circumstances that allow them to be successful. The program manager must establish such direction both within and outside the organization through a variety of means. Additionally, the program manager may have to accept calculated risk when he or she is unable to obtain clarity from the organization and then define clarity in his or her own terms. Accepting chaos, allowing chaos to exist, or passing down chaos all signal a lack of integrity and this does not create a culture conducive to successful projects.

The primary difference between a program manager and a project manager can be summed up in the words create and comply.

The program manager is responsible for creating the business environment culture the project manager complies with to execute. The degree of the program manager's direct control of that culture can vary, but through direct authority or organizational influence he or she is responsible for establishing the framework in which the project manager operates.

The project manager is judged on the triple constraint of time, cost, and scope of the project. The program manager also is judged on these three elements but at a level that is cumulative for all the projects and operations within the program. This aggregation of responsibilities for a variety of projects and operations means the program manager must make frequent trade-offs between business targets and project/operational performance.

Program management decisions are both tactical and strategic in nature. The strategy aspects of these decisions must consider multidimensional impacts beyond the near-term delivery dates of the project. Conversely, the project manager is challenged to deliver projects within the boundaries and framework established by the program manager. Typically, the project manager is and should be more delivery and execution focused whereas the program manager has to also be concerned with the overall health and effectiveness of the program over the long term.

The Ever-Changing Role of People and Technology

The fact is that today's program manager must execute programs effectively with two drivers that are in a constant state of change: people and technology. The team members, stakeholders, and project managers involved in executing the program today are likely not to be the same team members, stakeholders, and project managers supporting the program three to five years from now. People, for a variety of reasons, come and go in today's business environment. Therefore, organizations must have the ability to expand and/or contract on a rapid basis and react to changes in the marketplace. The ability to acquire people rapidly and make them valuable contributors quickly is a necessity for survival in today's marketplace.

The program manager must also deal with constant change in technology on a variety of fronts. Internal to the organization, as technology changes, every company has opportunities to improve operations. Additionally, there are usually active initiatives in various phases that can impact program execution: The company is going wireless. We are implementing an ERP system. They are changing the project management software standard. Technology is moving at such a pace that it is nearly impossible to predict the impact on the work environment five to ten years from now.

Consider the fax machine. When they first came out, they required special paper and a corresponding special machine to allow sending and receiving of documents. Today, I don't have a physical "fax machine" at all, but send faxes through my computer and receive them directly to my PDA with a virtual fax number. No machine necessary!

The companies that were able to adapt quickly as new faxing technology evolved were able to exploit the technology to increase organizational productivity. Externally, for the producers of fax machines, their program goals are in a constant state of change based on the current technology. That is, the products they make today will not be the products they make three years from now. Technology and the marketplace will not allow it.

Technology drives competition to the point that a valid program today may not be a valid program tomorrow in its current state. The internationally recognized inventor and futurist Ray Kurzweil, who developed Kurzweil's Law, the law of accelerating returns, states that the overall rate of technological progress is doubling approximately every decade. He concludes in his essay

"The Law of Accelerating Returns" that the twenty-first century will have about a thousand times the change as the twentieth century. Even if Kurzweil is partially correct, the rate of change will be phenomenal with tremendous impacts on business.

Consequently, today's technology does not have the "one-of-a-kind" staying power it once did. For example, in the 1960s, when Xerox came out with the copy machine, people didn't call the final copied product simply "a copy." It was a "Xerox copy." When someone had to photocopy something, they called it making a "Xerox." This terminology is still familiar today, over forty years later.

Technological advances today still exist, but overall, marketplace dominance doesn't tend to be as long-lasting. Once one company has a phone that can take pictures, for example, another company has the same feature within a matter of weeks or months. The exclusive technological breakthrough advantage that lasts for years is now a rarity. As a result, companies and organizations are under tremendous pressure to leverage technology internally to improve performance, and exploit technology externally to keep pace with market factors. The program manager is often at the focal point of this response.

Figures 1.1 and 1.2 show typical configurations for program management. Since all companies, nonprofits, and government organizations are unique in structure, no single diagram is representative of them all.

Figure 1.1 shows a program environment. The backdrop of the business environment consists of all the functions necessary to have a viable organization or company. It includes groups, such as sales, marketing, accounting, etc. We often have an overlap and interface between the business environment and the program environment. In fact, the program environment is a subset of the business environment. Programs can be small or range in size up to large business units. Programs may exist continually or they

FIGURE 1.1 Program Environment

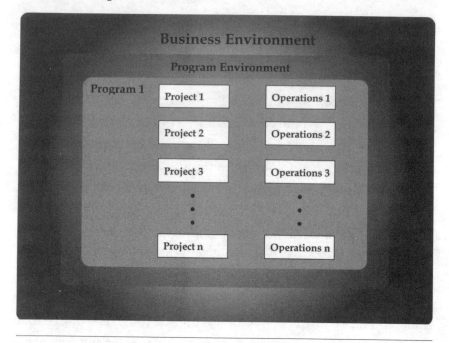

may have a defined endpoint. Most programs contain multiple projects that may be in various phases to improve operations or comply with external requirements or company strategy. Programs also usually contain numerous operations that are ongoing.

Figure 1.2 shows a representative operation with various projects that may be at work in support of the operation. New projects may continually be spawned as resources permit and/or existing projects are completed or new operations are created.

These diagrams illustrate some important, universal points:

- Most programs exist within a framework of overall business processes, such as human resources, purchasing, sales, marketing, logistics, etc.
- Multiple programs may share services or resources necessary to accomplish their objectives, or each program may be totally independent. (What is shared should be a strategic

decision made at the business level and should not happen haphazardly.)

- Multiple operations or projects within a program may share resources or services. (What is shared is a strategic decision made at the program level and should not happen haphazardly.) Operations can vary in size, from large operations where the projects are small in comparison with the operations, to no operations where projects dominate the program.
- As business needs dictate, new programs, operations, and projects may develop.

At this point it is important to note that some of the overall business processes can be classified as a program. For example, the director of the Human Resources department could also be a program manager responsible not only for ongoing operations in

FIGURE 1.2 Representative Operations with Support Projects

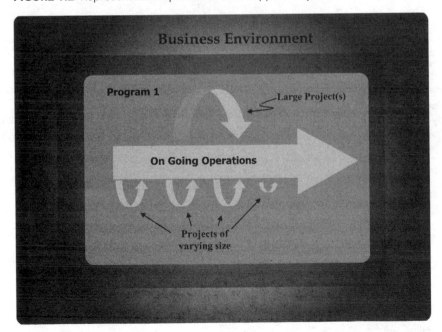

Human Resources, but also the development and delivery of new projects in support of Human Resources. Conversely, the director of the Human Resources department could just manage the organization and establish policy and not have the program manager functions or accountability.

With so many program models, the scope and responsibilities of program managers can vary significantly. Regardless, common threads remain, and one of those is the requirement to create and respond to change in a way that enables the program to meet or exceed its stated objectives. The need to create change through improving existing operations and/or deliver new projects and respond to changes such as government mandates like Sarbanes-Oxley, or implementation of Six Sigma management philosophy, creates a potentially unstable culture if it is not aggressively managed to ensure stability. Therefore, the program manager has to have processes that enable his or her organization to handle change successfully.

Creating the Ideal Program Management Culture

As we begin to form the ideal program management culture, the following definitions will help frame the chaos to clarity discussion.

Chaos—A state of extreme confusion and disorder
Accountability—Responsibility to someone or for some activity
Discipline—Implementation of a system of rules of
    conduct or method of practice
Clarity—Freedom from obscurity and ease of understanding
Accountability plus discipline equals integrity and
    results in clarity.

Further, Figure 1.3 illustrates the pyramid necessary for clarity to exist.

FIGURE 1.3 Program Management Pyramid

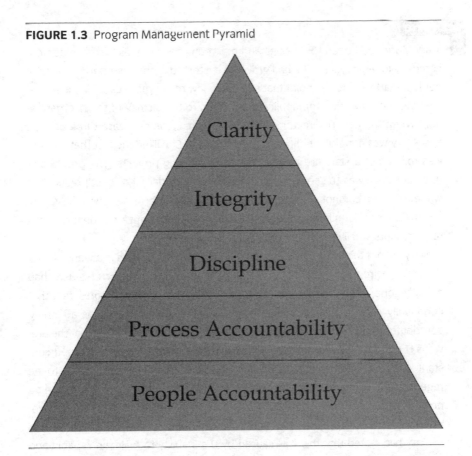

Chaos

I have spoken to and trained thousands of project managers. Most of them work in an environment filled with chaos. Project management is a profession where you must always be able to deal with change, because there is usually some degree of underlying change (i.e., technology and people) you cannot eliminate. However, this type of change is not what I mean by chaos. The chaos I am talking about results from a lack of knowledge, accountability, and discipline. Not only do a number of project managers work in environments that don't support their project management efforts, but these environments can also work against them.

Mary Moore had been VP of sales and marketing for a real estate development company for eight years. She had grown accustomed to the poor performance of her IT department to the point that she had a few of her more capable personnel creating their own desktop applications, much to the dismay of the IT organization. When the new IT director, Jennifer Johnson, came on board three months ago, Mary was hopeful for improved performance. She liked the fact that Jennifer was rolling out a standardized process for managing projects. The previous IT director's style was to see something he liked and declare it a "best practice" to whoever was in earshot without follow-up formally or informally. It was mass confusion. But now Jennifer's processes required her to prioritize her department's requirements and live with that priority for six months.

Mary did not think she could foresee requirements six months in advance in her dynamic environment. She could not believe that the company president had actually gone along with this strategy. Jennifer had convinced the president that continually changing requirements from all of IT's stakeholders was a leading contributor to the IT department's poor performance. Jennifer stated that the previous IT director never baselined requirements with customers. This caused constant upheaval in the projects because plans were continually having to be regenerated, ultimately causing the project teams to not take the planning process seriously. When you don't have a formalized plan, you don't have control. This resulted in project delays, cost overruns, and customer dissatisfaction.

Mary had stated that this was caused by IT's inability to maintain capable and motivated personnel, but Jennifer countered that the constantly changing requirements and chaos this caused contributed to the high turnover of capable personnel, who had options and wanted to work in an organization that had enough stability for their accomplishments to be meaningful. Additionally, her personnel were not following adequate change control processes in order to meet new demands with short deadlines, resulting in poor deliverables and causing lots of rework.

Mary was skeptical that stabilizing requirements would work, but she had direction from the president, and Jennifer had an impressive track record at her previous company. So she sat down with her team to establish and prioritize Sales and Marketing's requirements for the next six months. She could not believe that her requirements would then be weighed against the requirements of other VPs. This made her very uncomfortable, especially since she would have to sign off on her requirements.

In organizations that lack knowledge, accountability, and discipline at higher levels, there are always those who complain about results, but when forced to be accountable for their part of the process, they suddenly feel uncomfortable and under pressure. Often organizational leadership wants to have their cake and eat it too, and this is a significant contributor to project failure. Project managers in these kinds of environments are usually unnecessarily overworked and have little chance for success. A major advantage of processes for project management is that they drive accountability into the system at all levels. Therefore, program managers must apply leadership and strategy not only to make their program team accountable, but also to make external stakeholders and organizational leaders accountable.

A culture without an accepted and consistent method for delivering projects is simply not conducive to allowing project managers to be successful. The increasing popularity of project offices is in part an acknowledgment that the culture project managers work in determines their success as well as the project's success. Therefore, program managers need to continually create, manage, and improve the optimum culture. The establishment of a project management office is one way to try to achieve this culture.

Project Management Office

Today's project management offices may include the management of projects, or they may just be a policy-making entity. Some project management offices exist inside programs. In the case where project offices exist outside the program and have policy making authority, the program manager must negotiate with the project management office to ensure policies are adequate and not detrimental to the program. In the case where no project management office or policies exist, the program manager must establish his or her own policies and processes. This occurs most effectively when partnered with other program managers within the same organization. Project management offices must support program managers. Project management offices that forget this fundamental premise often create too many rules and policies that are not helpful. Processes, rules, and policies must be strategically rolled out in a manner that allows the organization to absorb and implement the changes. Everything that is right cannot be implemented immediately but must be implemented expediently.

This book addresses project management policy from a program manager's perspective because the program manager is ultimately accountable for delivery of the business objectives and adherence to the policy. Project management offices that establish policy as a primary function should be scaled down or phased out when that policy is mature. When these offices are not scaled down and/or do not have a close-out plan, they become a natural breeding ground for bureaucracy as they continue to try to justify their existence by continuing to create new policy. Additionally, leadership of a policy-based project management office should be rotated so the leader knows he or she will eventually have to go back into the organization and be successful with those policies.

I am a strong proponent of having people who create and verify policy at some point go out and execute and conform to the policies they created. It is risky to allow individuals who do not have to adhere, perform, and deliver within the guidelines they created to create new policies. Therefore, all policy positions in a project management office are best when temporary in nature, and the most effective people at setting policy are the eventual executers of that policy.

Chaotic Project Management Culture

Characteristics of a chaotic project management culture include:

- Having too many projects in work, exceeding organizational capacity

- Lacking a process to allow the creation and acceptance of new projects
- Having too many restrictive processes that prohibit the effective accomplishment of work
- Not having clearly defined or communicated goals, purpose, and/or mission
- Having priorities that are either always changing or incorrect or having no priorities
- Lacking process follow-through or not having processes at all
- Working amid unresolved resource conflicts
- Having unstable project and work schedules
- Having too many meetings
- Not having enough metrics to make good decisions, having too many metrics, or having no valid cost data
- Involving leadership in too many details
- Experiencing high turnover of personnel
- Having a small subset of project managers achieving most of the positive outcomes
- Encountering dissatisfied customers and stakeholders
- Following fads and always chasing the latest management trend as the panacea to all their current problems without sticking to any of them.

The characteristics of a chaotic project management culture often render the project manager ineffective. Therefore, the program manager's responsibility is to establish a culture that facilitates the accomplishment of projects. Unfortunately, through ignorance or a lack of commitment a lot of program managers neglect this responsibility, often at the expense of a shortsighted view that is focused on near-term problems and deliverables. Establishing a positive culture for project management requires a strategic plan and the discipline to stick to it.

Some program managers are playing chess—just focusing—on the short-term, next move; while others are playing seven steps ahead with the realization that this is just one of many games. As a result, many projects fail because of the environment the project manager works in rather than because of inappropriate action by the project manager. Bad or nonexistent program management is a primary cause of failed projects.

Accountability

Two levels of accountability are critical to establishing a culture of clarity that fulfills project management initiatives with repeated successes. The first level of accountability is having someone who is accountable for the establishment, improvement, and compliance with the project management process itself.

In some companies, one individual defines project management processes. This person may be the head of a project/program office, head a major program within the company, or serve as chief information officer, chief technology officer, chief project officer, or chief engineer. Other companies may be of a scale where the project management processes are not the same across large segments of the organization. Each program manager or organizational head may have full discretion to define the process or establish his or her own process over a broad framework.

The second level of accountability involves clearly defining all roles and responsibilities for project managers, team members, consultants, and project office personnel. This is challenging, because each person must be able to maintain this clarity as the organization expands, contracts, accepts new projects, implements new technology, and reassigns personnel. The program manager has to aggressively ensure the integrity of clear roles and accountability as everything around him or her is shifting and twisting.

Developing accountability begins with selling the workforce on the concept that project management is best accomplished through a structured, repeatable process. These processes are then created and rolled out in an orderly fashion to ensure acceptance and to minimize disruption of existing work activities. Most people agree that implementing every process that is logical, right, and valuable immediately or all at once overwhelms the organization. Therefore, the program manager must prioritize these processes based on the challenges the organization is facing, and then establish a strategy for implementing the processes. Strong accountability practice includes establishing an individual accountable for managing each process.

Discipline

Do we always follow the logical, well-thought-out planned process we have established for repeatable success? Or do we short-circuit the process every time an imminent deadline, cost pressure, or a demanding customer or stakeholder surfaces? I am not advocating you never violate logical, well-thought-out planned processes that ensure repeatable success. But when you do, you must have a process that approves such a deviation and publicly acknowledges it to all. When you handle process violations properly, you signal to the entire project management community within the organization that we will act with integrity when under pressure.

While these violations should be rare, they are very important because they help you improve the process. How? These process violations are, in fact, signals that the process may need to be improved, and as such, you must view process violations as opportunities for process improvement. Exercise due diligence with regard to each process violation's root cause. I once worked with a program manager who would always say, "We have improved our processes one failure at a time."

The most important word in program management success is "integrity." Do you act with integrity? People know if you don't.

It is ironic that when companies perform assessments to learn why a project failed, they rarely cite "lack of integrity" as the reason. However, lack of integrity is a leading cause of project failure and program management headaches, along with lack of effective program management. That is, poor program management practices do not instill or maintain discipline, and this results in a lack of integrity. Accountability plus discipline equals integrity and results in clarity. Lack of integrity is a sign of an immature project management organization or an immature program manager. Lack of integrity at the program management level contributes to a chaotic project management culture.

You may be in a level of management where the pay is good and accountability entails tremendous self-discipline—the type of self-discipline that requires a focus on the process that accomplishes projects rather than the work of the projects itself. This requires a long-term view—something many program managers lack. Some program managers are too operations-focused, some are too detail-focused, some are too self-centered and career-focused, and some are too customer-focused. Over-focus on any one of the aforementioned can cause the program manager to ignore the strong process focus he or she must have.

If you are a program manager reading this book, examine your schedule from last week. Assess the percentage of time you spent on improving the process of accomplishing work versus the work itself. The familiar trap of being too busy fighting fires to spend any time preventing fires is common. Also, some of the managers at this level got there through their heroic effort of being able to wade through the chaos and successfully deliver projects. This prior success often makes them susceptible to jumping into troubled projects, spending their precious time on remediation rather than ensuring that valid processes are in place that help eliminate the need for remediation in the first place.

Achieving Discipline with Minimal Processes

During dinner with a senior executive from a Fortune 100 company, I brought up the importance of project management processes. The senior executive agreed with me about the importance of a structured project management process, but stated that his company's strategy was to deploy as few processes as possible because of the overhead and high potential for bureaucracy that exists with processes. Additionally, the varied nature of their global operations made consistency in process problematic.

He explained that he would select a relatively young person (out of college less than five years), take him or her to a foreign country, and give the person a major project assignment in that foreign location. He would then get on a plane and leave the project manager there. His role then was to continually travel the globe, meeting with and mentoring these project managers, and then report back to headquarters for strategic discussion and remediation plans. Then he'd start the process all over again.

The global and somewhat sporadic nature of his company's operations makes it difficult to establish and enforce a standardized project management methodology given the broad range of subcontractors with varying capabilities, different cultures, political risk, and government regulations. Therefore, the streamlined process they employed is one of frequent and structured mentoring, where the executive provides mentoring through periodic visits and assessments.

An advantage of his company's method is that when his project managers are in mid-career with ten-plus years of experience under their belt in that environment, they are extremely capable and have the ability to independently handle complex projects with a high level of confidence. Unfortunately, everyone does not respond well to the intense pressure of working with a high level of responsibility and accountability without the support of a lot of processes.

As this executive visits his project managers, he is there to detect and prevent meltdowns of the project, the project manager, or both. Unfortunately, with this method he sometimes has a few egregious project failures, but overall he is pleased with the process because the company is able to react quickly with a minimum of overhead and they have a cadre of senior project managers who are highly capable of working independently in a variety of global environments. He also mentioned that they did extensive interviewing and had comprehensive screening processes to ensure the people they hired were not only highly capable, but could also handle the pressure and travel their company required.

At first glance, you could conclude that this company has no program or project management processes, at least not as the Project Management Institute's Project Management Body of Knowledge and other organizations have defined them. In fact, the contrary is true. This company has made a conscious decision to have little, if any, consistency in process among project managers in order to minimize overhead and deal with the wide-ranging assortment of projects and venues their company faces. Based on that decision, they have a disciplined process whereby a senior executive/program manager frequently meets, mentors, and assesses each project manager. They also have a rigorous hiring process to select employees who can excel in this type of environment, and they indoctrinate them into their system directly from college. These are all processes—albeit people-dependent ones. (We will discuss striking a strategic balance between people and process in Chapter 4.)

The key part of their process is the conscious decision not to have a detailed, structured methodology and then establishing the factors that would make them successful without one. This is what separates this company from the many other organizations that don't have a structured methodology. You can have a process without a structured methodology, but unfortunately most organizations without a structured methodology have done so haphazardly without due diligence and do not have a disciplined process that ensures repeatable success.

Staying True to Your Process

Multiple models assess project management process maturity, but like a lot of project management in vogue today, the definitions and assessments are more complicated and detailed than necessary. Project management is simply the application and execution of structured, organized, common sense.

To avoid spending hundreds of thousands of dollars on consultants and sophisticated assessments, answer the following three questions.

1. Do we have a process?
2. Do we follow the process to accomplish the work?
3. Do we improve the process?

In summary, do you act with integrity and do what your process documentation says you should? If you can answer "yes" to all three questions just posed, you have an organization that acts with integrity (accountability and discipline). If your organization is not acting with integrity, you have a program management issue.

SCENARIO

During a project management class for the Information Technology division for a major retailer, the subject of processes came up. To my surprise, the discussion among the participants became very heated, centering on whether the organization had processes for project management. The bottom line was that processes were in place, but people didn't always use them to accomplish the project work activities, to the degree that some personnel didn't even know the processes existed. During the discussion it quickly became clear that we had three distinct groups of people in the room: those who knew there were processes and followed them, those who knew there were processes and didn't follow them, and those who had no idea there were processes at all. Unfortunately, this kind of disparity can be commonplace. The program manager must identify and assess such disparities and deploy strategies to rectify them to ensure program integrity.

Seeking Clarity

Company culture, organization culture, program culture, and project culture . . . when all of these cultures exist in harmony with one another, you have the greatest opportunity for effective project delivery because you have intense clarity. Frequently, these cultures do not exist in congruence or harmony, and that puts the greatest amount of responsibility and pressure on the program manager. The program manager often exists on a business level and must interface with business-level processes while establishing and enforcing project-level processes. Therefore, the program manager has to seamlessly exist in all these cultures and work to establish congruence among them.

Earlier we defined clarity as "freedom from obscurity and ease of understanding." From a program manager's perspective, clarity is defined by clear objectives for success, clear lines of accountability, and adherence to established processes.

The number-one enemy of the program manager that is a result of not having clarity is apathy. Apathy occurs when the chaos in the organization reaches a point where individuals feel their effort doesn't matter, is wasted, or is severely hampered. People become apathetic and just go through the motions without passion, energy, or a sense of purpose. All of the aforementioned characteristics of a chaotic program management culture are contributors to an apathetic worker or team.

The accountability of the project managers for the triple constraint—delivering on time, within budget, and within the agreed-upon scope—is clear and self-evident, even though they often have to work diligently with stakeholders for clarification of these constraints.

Fix the Cause of the Problem

When thrust into my first position of real responsibility, I sought the advice of many respected leaders in the organization. No advice proved more valuable than the statement: "Kill what's ugly while it's young." "Ugly" is the enemy of clarity. Ugly is the root cause of chaos.

At first I was taken aback by this statement, but there is tremendous wisdom and power in it as a management mantra. Consider this: Have you ever worked or been associated with an organization that had problems everywhere, but they all seemed too big to solve? Almost everyone has. Many times, the majority of these problems didn't start too big to solve; rather, people within the company allowed them to grow and become larger and more intertwined. Eventually, the problem reached the point where it took more than one person, one department, or one business unit to solve, making its elimination a much greater challenge. This is amplified when processes exist in the work environment that do not have single points of accountability for the process. No one is accountable and it seems no one can fix the problem.

To kill what's ugly while it's young, you must first be on the hunt for ugly. You must have processes in place that bring ugly to you. You must identify the root cause of ugly. Many good leaders fear those problems that lie beneath the radar. Program personnel may not bring them out to light for fear of reprisal, or they have the cavalier attitude that this is not important enough for anyone to know about. That's why the program manager must have processes in place that quickly surface problems so the company can resolve them.

I knew of one program manager who had "Confession Friday." You could bring him any problem, miscue, or mix-up on Friday and he promised to deliver a good attitude. He would even jokingly say, "All sins are forgiven thee." This method had a way of ensuring that there was nothing ugly out there lurking in the organization for more than one week. If you had a problem older than one week that he should have been aware of, that meant you had missed confession and better have good justification for why. You did not want to miss confession.

Once you define ugly, you must kill it. The good news is that you have many choices of death for ugly; however, all the choices boil down to two primary methods: execution or starvation. Execution involves terminating the unproductive activity or process immediately or after some appropriate time period, usually tied to an event or milestone. Starvation involves not feeding the bad activity or process by establishing alternate means to circumvent what's ugly. Sometimes you can accomplish these things immediately, but frequently it takes time to rid the organization of an ugly characteristic.

There is nothing wrong with having a two-year or multiyear plan to alleviate a problem if that's how long it takes. The point is that you must implement a strategy and plan; otherwise, the problem continues to resurface and spawn new problems. Without a plan to alleviate problems, apathy develops, as workers feel forced to deal with obvious problems yet see no plan or effort toward their resolution. Even worse, many ugly processes have a way of growing over time, and when there is a problem with a process, people tend to work outside the process to accomplish work, or they "bandage" the process. Years and years of bandage remedies without a cure result in problems that seem intractable (entrenched ugly) and often create new problems with unforeseen consequences.

Program managers face many problems and challenges on a daily basis. Some of these problems and challenges require longer-term solutions. Ultimately, minimizing the program manager's problems and challenges requires a focus on the process and culture of how project management is accomplished. Remember that accountability plus discipline equals integrity and results in clarity. Clarity is the goal.

Chaos to Clarity

1. The program manager must create, manage, and continually improve the project management culture.
2. A program manager is first and foremost a leader.
3. Technology drives competition to the point that a valid program today may not be a valid program tomorrow in its current state.
4. There are always those who complain about results, but who, when forced to be accountable for their part of the process, suddenly feel uncomfortable and under pressure.
5. A major advantage of processes for project management is that they drive accountability into the system at all levels.
6. Establishing a positive culture for project management requires a strategic plan and the discipline to stick to it.
7. Many projects fail because of the environment the project manager works in rather than any inappropriate action of the project manager.
8. The program manager has to aggressively ensure the integrity of clear roles and accountability as everything around him or her is shifting and twisting.
9. When you handle process violations properly, you signal to the entire project management community within the organization that we will act with integrity when under pressure.
10. The number-one enemy of the program manager that is a result of not having clarity is apathy.
11. The message of "Kill what's ugly while it's young" is simple: Fix the root cause of problems and fix them early.

Attributes of the Effective Program Manager

Nonstandardized terms, the same terms with different meanings, and different terms with the same meaning, have plagued the project management field for decades. Recently, the Project Management Institute's Project Management Body of Knowledge has made great strides in defining standardized terminology and processes for the field of project management. Nevertheless, ambiguities still abound. Therefore, for clarity with regard to this book, we will define project management and program management as follows:

- Project management is management of a group of activities or initiatives with a defined deliverable and a definite starting point and end point.

- Program management is management of a group of projects and/or operations to achieve business targets, goals, or strategies, and may or may not have a defined end point.

Unlike projects, programs may never end or end only when the business's needs or organizational strategy changes. Programs have a higher level of complexity than projects, involve more and higher-level stakeholders, utilize more resources, have more conflict, and require more coordination.

The Program Manager's Role

A program manager's job is very demanding, to say the least. Typically, a program manager is subjected to all the complexities and stresses of a project manager, plus is required to manage ongoing operations while meeting business goal targets for the month, quarter, or year. The program manager often has to strike a balance between the amount of resources spent on operations and the amount of resources spent on development and new projects. Being a program manager requires a greater skill set and more diverse background than being a project manager.

A program manager needs to have an ingrained sense of organizational mission, must lead and have the presence of a leader, must have a vision and strategy for long-term organizational improvement, must be a relationship builder, and must have the experience and ability to assess people and situations beyond their appearances.

The preceding attributes need to be combined with strong analytical skills, the ability to be tough-minded, and the know-how permitting the program manager to find a myriad of paths and means to accomplish program objectives. Ultimately, the program manager must develop a culture of success while being a program champion.

As the main program champion, the program manager needs to garner resources and use his or her relationship capital to pave the way for the program to be successful. Relationship capital is the amount of influence a program manager can wield through the organization by establishing relationships of ever-increasing trust, internal and external to the organization. In this role as program champion, the program manager is always selling the program's importance to the company's stakeholders and team members. This selling involves an in-depth knowledge of the organization, including how the program fits into the organization, and how the company establishes program goals, as well as the plans and initiatives required to meet those goals. Clear understanding on all these items is essential. The program manager, in the role of program champion, must constantly communicate the program, its purpose, and why it is valuable to the organization.

Often when promoted from technology professional to project manager, the individual is ill prepared to utilize the variety of skills required to be successful at the project level. That's because the technical professional often lacks the interpersonal, communication, and organizational skills necessary to be project manager. Equally significant and with more risk to the organization is the hurdle between project manager and program manager. This hurdle requires the project manager (now program manager) to think with a business focus and manage both process and culture. Since a project has a defined end date while a program is usually continual and includes ongoing operations, the challenges are greater and the stakes are higher.

SCENARIO

For example, consider Ralph. Ralph had been an excellent project manager in his area of technical expertise. He had been with the company for only two years but had extensive project management experience and training with his previous employer and was a certified project manager. Ralph was excited when he was selected to be program manager and thought he understood the scope of his new duties as program manager. But after one month in his new role, Ralph realized how sedate his previous role as project manager had been, even though it seemed dynamic and demanding at the time. Ralph now had eight project managers, two operations managers, and a few support personnel working for him.

Feeling overwhelmed, he wrote out the following challenges he was now facing:

1. There is constant fighting over resources internal to this program and external with other programs.
2. There is little if any teamwork.
3. Two of the project managers are new and require high levels of guidance.
4. One of the experienced project managers is perceived as abrasive by the customer.
5. The company has given different cost targets twice in one month that have no perceived basis of rationale.
6. Sales personnel have made a few promises the team can't fulfill, requiring us to accept additional risk and do damage control.
7. I spend a quarter of my time in company business meetings that don't seem to relate directly to the program.
8. The company is in the process of rolling out a new enterprise-wide software system that is consuming program resources, and they keep trying to borrow one of my best people.
9. The VP has a pet project he wants worked that is not in the plan and doesn't contribute to the cost targets.
10. Every project manager is collecting and presenting status in a different way based on their preferences and/or stakeholder requirements.
11. Priority is given to the most current "perceived" need, often to who is yelling the loudest or whispering to the right person without consideration of all planned activities.
12. Project risks are not collected and/or communicated well, resulting in surprises that are contributing to a lack of trust with stakeholders.
13. The team could benefit substantially from training but they are so busy working and fighting fires, they don't seem to have time for training or process improvement.

As stated earlier, the most significant difference between project manager responsibility and program manager responsibility is the requirement for the program manager to establish a culture of success. This culture is based on process. Without this culture, few programs or projects will have sustainable success. Some of

Ralph's challenges above can be temporarily alleviated in the short term, but the long-term cure requires process and culture change that will occur only through strong leadership and applied strategy.

Program Success Factors

What makes some program managers consistently successful and others consistently marginal or average? Before we dive into this question, let's detail what characterizes a successful program. The key factors are:

- Stability of operations and operations becoming more efficient
- A proper, strategically identified balance between operations and development/new projects
- Projects delivered on time and on budget
- Clear lines of accountability
- Stable, well-understood budget process
- Professional growth of program personnel
- Clear, well-understood project management and decision processes
- Clear objectives for success
- Happy stakeholders
- Constant alignment with the strategic or organizational vision

All of the above are a subset or result of the culture the program manager must develop. A positive, supportive, structured culture makes programs self-regulating and success automatic.

The program manager is, in essence, an icon. As the icon, he or she serves as the focal point for the entire program, and others imitate his or her behavior, both the good and the bad. Therefore, the program manager must always remain cognizant that in this role of leader, he or she sets the organization's tone. If the program manager is noncritical, the organization is likely to be noncritical. If the program manager is a screamer, the organization is likely to scream. If the program manager is enthusiastic, the organization is likely to be enthusiastic. Whatever trait the leader displays seeps into the organization over time.

The Program Manager as a Leader

The following leadership traits, combined with an aggressive management approach, ensure success at the program level. These traits include: presence, relationship building, consistency, effective questioning, decision making, and mentoring. While every program manager must possess these traits, equally important is that the organization possesses these traits. And since the program manager is responsible for developing a culture with these traits, he or she must demonstrate them on a daily basis.

Presence

Presence is often a requirement and a sought-after trait for executives. Some executive coaches teach presence, as it is usually a factor organizations consider when selecting future leaders. Unfortunately, many people mistakenly undervalue the importance of presence. A human resources director for a leading telecommunications company once told me she is always looking internally at the company's high achievers and top performers. The ones with presence are put on the fast track. For our purposes, we will define presence as the ability to appear or outwardly demonstrate the characteristics of a leader.

The program manager is the very symbol of the program and all of the leader's actions reflect outwardly and inwardly on the program itself.

- Outward reflection is the perception the program manager creates with external stakeholders. Therefore, the program manager must create and manage perception and not leave it to chance, because external stakeholders, such as customers, other business units, and organizational leadership often judge the program manager's behaviors. Others must perceive the program manager as a leader who is in control of the program and receptive to the needs of external stakeholders. If this perception is lacking, external stakeholders may attempt to work around the program manager and thus undermine his or her authority, limiting the program manager's effectiveness.

- Inward reflection is the perception the program manager creates internal to the program, and those internal to the program tend to copy the behaviors. So if the program manager effectively employs the other traits described in this chapter, then he or she is in effect instilling these traits into the organization, and this can pay huge dividends, including minimizing the amount of intervention the program manager must make at lower levels and projects because his or her subordinates are already executing in a manner the program manager finds successful.

Ultimately, leaders want their organizations to be self-regulating, as such an organization allows the leader time to focus on the more demanding challenges and opportunities while the organization "self-regulates" the majority of activities. Often the program manager misses opportunities because he or she is too bogged down dealing with issues in the program that should be self-regulating. Some program managers never excel because they cannot release control of the day-to-day activities that should be self-regulating.

Self-regulation takes time to create, but it is the ultimate definition of presence. With self-regulation, the organization acts and performs just like the program manager would want it to even if he or she is not present. The program team intrinsically thinks like the program manager, and everyone knows what is expected of them: Clarity.

Relationship Building

Program management involves human relationships, and the program manager must be more than proficient at relationship building. There was a character "Joe Friday" from the TV show *Dragnet*. He was famous for the statement "Just the facts, ma'am." However, leadership is more than "just the facts." It's about establishing relationships of trust "up and out" (meaning to and among stakeholders) and "down and in" (meaning to and among teams and project managers).

Leadership exists on a basis of trust, and program managers must constantly develop and use relationship capital. Given the number of relationships that exist at the program level, program managers must establish strategies and tactics to manage these relationships. Suppliers, customers, subcontractors, program personnel, auditors, etc., all require strong relationships, as these all facilitate honest dialogue and result in quick problem-identification and -resolution. Additionally, these relationships instill a sense of loyalty and friendship that you can leverage in a time of crisis or need. Performance in a time of crisis or need is highly dependent on the trust that existed within the team prior to the crisis or need.

Many program managers use formal methods, such as surveys, interviews, complaint logs, and focus groups, to constantly analyze and assess the status of critical relationships. Why is this important? Consider this: Being able to accelerate a deliverable can be more dependent on your personal r with the supplier than the contractual relationship that c. between you and the supplier. Likewise, customer satisfaction is often dependent on the strength of your relationship with the customer. And the ability to increase your team's productivity is often dependent on your personal relationship with the team. In short, the ability to accomplish objectives through others is directly correlated to the strength of the relationships or the relationship capital the program manager has developed.

One of the best leadership tips I ever received was to read books on salesmanship. You may be wondering what sales and leadership have in common. Through various sales books, I've learned that the best salespeople are actually great relationship builders. Relationship building involves knowing your customers, understanding what motivates them, what their needs are, and how to negotiate and communicate with them in a way that allows you to best meet their needs. This information is equally valuable to the program manager, as we lead better through relationships than with logic. With solid and productive relationships, we can then implement logic within the program.

The following sales books are invaluable resources for the program manager:

- *How to Win Friends and Influence People* by Dale Carnegie
- *How I Raised Myself from Failure to Success in Selling* by Frank Bettger
- *Selling the Invisible* by Harry Beckwith

Another advantage of building relationships is that it facilitates the ability to solve problems. For example, many companies struggle with fixing entrenched problems that cross organizational boundaries because they don't have respected leaders with relationship capital that can cross those boundaries. Without deep-rooted trust on all levels, program managers will have a hard time fixing or changing the problem. And deep-rooted trust is relationship-based. To be a successful program manager, you must have deep-rooted trust across the organization. Only then can you leverage relationships to solve those persistent problems that plague the company.

As a program manager, you must encourage your project and operations managers to be relationship builders as well. An organization with a high percentage of relationship builders is an organization that can solve problems quickly and respond to new challenges effectively. The right response for solving problems will often become self-evident. The ability of organizations to implement this response is dependent on relationship builders who can leverage trust to overcome the natural and political resistance to change in the organization.

Consistency

When I say "consistency," I am not advocating that all program managers act the same. What I mean is that whatever style, management techniques, or leadership traits you employ—implement them consistently. The program manager must be predictable, as consistency and predictability are positive traits that provide stability for the organization. Programs are often very dynamic, involving a virtual whirlwind of change, and the leader must provide stability "anchors" wherever possible. Consistency in style, management techniques, and leadership traits are important anchors for any organization and contribute to a stable work environment. If you have ever had the unfortunate opportunity to work with or for, or to observe a leader who is inconsistent, you can attest to the frustration and problematic nature of the work environment the inconsistent leader creates.

Inconsistent leaders sometimes require a lot of detail, and on other occasions require little detail. Sometimes they want you to seek their approval, then later question why you brought the same kind of approval request to them. Sometimes they give permission to speak to external stakeholders and sometimes they don't. The bottom line is the people working for inconsistent leaders often spend unnecessary time wondering how to proceed or harboring resentment because they cannot predict what the leader wants.

Consider the quote from Gracian in the book *The Art of Worldly Wisdom:* "A wise person is always consistent in his best qualities, and because of this he gets the credit of trustworthiness. If he changes, he does so for good reason and after good consideration."

Be Trustworthy. Consistency begins with trust. Are you trustworthy? Do you fulfill your commitments? Trust is the foundation of successful leadership, and you must first be trustworthy and then accept the challenge to create ever-increasing relationships of trust between you and your organization and among the organization members themselves. Trust doesn't happen automatically. It happens over time, presuming individuals are trustworthy. Team-building initiatives, whether formal team meetings or informal group activities, can accelerate the development of trust.

Define Expectations. Consistency also means defining expectations. Let people know what they can expect from you and what you expect from them. Recognize that you are not exhibiting trust if you violate the expectations you give others. Often leaders idealistically overpromise concerning goals they aspire to but have not yet achieved. A classic and often repeated example is the leader who advertises an "open-door" policy. This leader states that he or she will always listen, but from the team's perspective, although the door may always be open, the leader is usually not there on the other side of it, and when he or she is there, it never seems to be a good time to talk. Do not overpromise about things you may not be able to deliver. When you do not deliver what you promised, others will view your actions as a violation of trust.

TIP

I advocate a "cracked door" policy. Establish a set time every day when people can come and see you informally. It can be early in the morning or late in the day or during the lunch hour. Whatever time you choose, make sure the organization knows about it. I once worked for a high-level leader who was always available between 6:30 a.m. and 7:30 a.m. to whoever stopped by. You might have to eat breakfast with him or wait your turn, but he would be there, first come first served regardless of organizational rank. He would essentially be unavailable the remainder of the day unless you were on his calendar.

Establish Personal Rules. The famous basketball player Michael Jordan was so good that opposing teams created what became known as "The Jordan Rules." These were a set of rules they would apply to try to contain him. I recommend that you establish a set of rules for yourself that you make your team aware of. For example, when a new team member joins my program or I have a new program, I will provide the following overall rules as guidance when it comes to working with and for me.

1. I am a recovered "control freak" and have occasional lapses. I will ask for your forgiveness.
2. I will always treat you professionally and I expect the same.
3. I don't like long e-mails, presentations, or meetings. Get to the point.
4. I will always remain calm unless you are working or allowing work outside of the change control process. (This is my number one pet peeve, especially when it comes to verbal promises to the customer.)
5. Meetings should start on time and have an agenda.
6. Try to keep me from being surprised by the customer, leadership, and peers. Be on the lookout for issues with political ramifications.

7. If you need me to make a decision and I am unavailable, Ralph Jones can act on my behalf and I will stand by his decision.
8. Err on the side of aggressiveness. I forgive aggressive mistakes. I don't like passive mistakes.
9. I will always question you to ensure thoroughness. The longer we work together, the less I question unless there is a problem.

Those are my preferences and style. Yours will differ. The key is to make others aware of your preferences and style so they can quickly adapt with a minimum of time spent trying to figure you out. Describe yourself as you are and not as you want to be. We are not perfect. You may even lead the list with one or more negative trait(s). We all have them. You must know what yours are.

Explain Inconsistencies. Finally, let your team know that on rare occasions you may have to be consistently inconsistent. In other words, circumstances may arise that require that you deviate from your usual course of action. For instance, you may not be able to grant the same freedom/authority level to a project manager with two years' worth of experience that you would to a project manager with thirteen years of experience. Recognize that when you have to be inconsistent, you must offer extra communication to explain the inconsistencies; otherwise, trust questions will arise. (Know that just because your team doesn't verbalize these questions, this does not mean they don't silently harbor them.)

Effective Questioning

Effective questioning starts with being perceptive and in touch with the organization—having a feel for the organization above and beyond what charts and graphs provide. While guidelines for asking productive questions do exist, good questions often result from a good feel for what's going on. For example, any capable university professor can tell by a student's question whether he or she has read the assignment and whether the student is "up to speed" on the subject. Similarly, your program team can tell how in touch you are with the program by the quality of the questions you ask. Your team assesses you based on the quality of your questions. Realize that you do not have to have expertise in the technology or line of business to be assigned as a program manager or project manager within that technology or line of business. Once assigned, however, you must completely and aggressively immerse yourself in the organization's culture, its technology, and its line of business.

Good questioning starts with listening, not just to your direct reports, but also to the entire organization. In Steven Covey's book *Seven Habits of Highly Effective People*, habit number five is to seek first to understand. From a program management perspective, listening and understanding are prerequisites of good questioning. It is valuable to pay attention to not only what individuals are telling you, but also to what the process is telling you. Look at the process and culture as entities and then listen to what they are saying.

As a consultant, I identify and solve problems for organizations. I know that 80 percent of this role involves listening to individuals, and observing the process and the culture. Both the problem and the solution are usually already there. I just have to carefully listen for them. Systems that include humans and human interactions (organizations) are complicated, and it is easy and tempting to come to quick solutions that may temporarily alleviate a problem and not cure it. Effective questioning should lead to cures. You may still have to apply temporary fixes, as cures may take time, but the cure has to be part of the plan.

From the program manager's perspective, we need to recognize that our project managers, direct reports, and stakeholders may filter what they provide us. While part of their job is indeed to filter what they provide us, their filtering process is not always perfect. Therefore, to ensure that information is unfiltered or is filtered according to our intentions, we must periodically get into the nooks and crannies of the organization to see with our own eyes and hear with our own ears. The higher the level you reach in an organization, or the larger the program, the more obstacles there are that limit your opportunity to listen and talk with people at the working level. A challenging schedule, secretary, private conference room, and scattered teams can make this problematic. However, no amount of difficulty can discount the necessity or importance of reaching out to these people.

Some leaders rarely leave their office or personal conference room unless they are going to see someone more important than themselves. As a result, their view of the organization, based on filtered reports and data, can become more and more skewed and abstract over time. This shows up in the content of their questions. I'm amazed at how often some leaders will ask a question, and the rest of the room immediately recognizes that the leader has no idea how things are really accomplished at the working level. These leaders are displaying a trait that is the very opposite of being perceptive and observant. They are attempting to lead without a true feel for the pulse of the organization, and this causes them to lose credibility. As General Sam Phillips, who served as director of NASA's Apollo program, once said, "Regardless of how scientific our approach to problem solving might be and regardless of how sophisticated our management systems and tools might become, a program will never be managed without the effective usage of this 'eyeball-to-eyeball' communications mode."

This is why you must inform your direct reports and project managers that you can and will talk to anyone at any time who is involved in the program. While your intent isn't to circumvent their authority, you must have a feel to lead appropriately. No matter how busy or demanding your schedule, you must spend a little bit of time each day obtaining this feel.

TIP

Utilize your list of all personnel involved in the program and use a random number generator like the one found in Microsoft Excel. (The RAND function in Excel will allow you to create a random number for each person.) Sort on this number and an individual's name will appear at the top. If the person indicated is in your vicinity, go talk to him or her face-to-face. If he or she is outside of your area, call the person on the phone. You don't even have to discuss program business. Personal communication with all levels of the team is the goal. You obtain a feel just by communicating with the person directly. This interaction also sows seeds of trust. It expresses your concern for the integrity of the organization at all levels. Doing this daily, at random, ensures that you will not overlook areas considered noncritical where problems, issues, and opportunities are often lying in wait. Do not underestimate the power of selecting people at random. What you learn from these random calls will tell you far more over time.

An effective technique to employ when speaking to these personnel identified at random is to occasionally ask, "If we could do one thing better or fix one thing, what would it be?" Be careful not to overreact to people's recommendation; rather, use the information they reveal as a basis for getting the whole story, or seeing the entire picture painted. Doing so also lets your entire leadership chain know they cannot selectively filter information or frame issues and decisions in a manner that is not reflective of the true situation. If you have never done this, you will be amazed at the results after six months. Becoming more visible will also make you more perceptive and in tune with the organization's challenges. Such structured listening to the organization provides a sound basis for asking good questions.

TIP

Here are some additional guidelines for asking good questions:

- Beginning questions with "how" or "what" causes less defensiveness than using "why" openings.

- Defensiveness often occurs because of what we communicate nonverbally, and we must be careful to keep our emotions in check and remain positive.
- Show patience by waiting for a response to your question.
- Ask only one question at a time.
- Use silence strategically to draw out more information. People are uncomfortable with silence, and by being silent you can cause a person to provide additional information.
- Instead of "yes" or "no" questions, ask open-ended questions, such as "How do you feel about . . . ?" "Tell me more about . . ." "What else can we do about. . . ?" and "If we could make this perfect, what would have to happen?"

Questioning is a critical element toward establishing a culture of thoroughness. The words you never want to hear or have to say in the work environment are: "We didn't think about that."

Questioning is a skill and a beautiful thing to watch if you get to observe a master practitioner. Their skill at ferreting out key issues is amazing, and their thoroughness in asking questions results in thoroughness on the part of the organization. No one wants to appear unprepared when presenting to leaders who are effective questioners, and that's how your team members should feel. They must have a mind-set of "I better take care of this because I know he or she is going to ask me about it." Essentially, you want your team answering your questions before you ask them. That's self-regulation.

Decision Making

Effective decision making is a trait all successful program managers possess. Once again, like a lot of traits needed for program success, decision making is a process that affects program culture. Many organizations fail or stumble along because it takes too long for personnel to get the decisions they need. Program managers not only must resolve conflicts quickly, but also must make timely decisions with regard to strategy and tactical implications that affect the program. Causes for the delay in decision making can include:

- A chaotic environment where the personnel needing a decision have to struggle to get on the decision maker's calendar
- A lack of clear criteria for when the decision needs to be escalated. The decision maker then spends too much time on decisions that should be made at lower levels, and decisions that should be escalated remain hidden too long.
- Lack of accountability

Problems are naturally a part of every program, and the unexpected occasionally happens. Risks do materialize. Murphy's Law still exists. The program manager should not be surprised when any of the aforementioned occur and should block out time on his or her calendar daily to handle these unexpected events. Typically, early morning and/or late afternoon are the best times for decision making. Why? Because now you have up to two windows of opportunity daily in which decisions can be made. As an added advantage, this process stabilizes your calendar. And when your calendar is stable, you have the opportunity to stabilize the calendar of all those reporting to you. When the project managers' and operations managers' calendars are more stable, the teams' calendar becomes more stable and productive. This contributes to a culture of stability.

TIP

Many people work in environments in which they must juggle meetings and events on a daily basis because of changes in the leader's calendar. Having a set time daily to handle the inevitable problem or issue is a good strategy for maintaining a stable culture. For example, if I know you have thirty minutes to an hour blocked off every day at 9 a.m. and 3 p.m., I don't have to go through the hassle of trying to schedule you for a special meeting. I simply contact your secretary or assistant and get on the agenda, which is prioritized before the meeting. If the agenda is empty, then no meeting takes place. If you are unavailable at that time, empower someone to act on your behalf.

As a program manager, you must establish a culture where decisions get made quickly and at the appropriate level. This requires clear lines of accountability and escalation processes to bubble up decisions to the appropriate level. In an aggressive decision approach, all of the data the decision maker would need is typically not available. The alternative of waiting on information is tempting, but often the information is slower to arrive than anticipated. And when it does arrive, it may just confirm the original decision plan.

More often than not, you are better off making decisions when you have most of the data and not wait until you have all of the data.

One caveat for consideration is some advice I received from a seasoned program manager. He always used to say: "Be wary of the first reports received about any major circumstances positive or negative." His experience was that there are always a few individuals in the organization who want to be the first to share "breaking news," and these people occasionally don't have all the facts, don't have the facts in proper alignment, or embellish the facts they do have. Another program manager calls it the "Geraldo Factor" after the infamous news reporter. So caution is in order with first reports.

Making decisions quickly also means that some decisions will not be correct. This is okay, as long as you rapidly rectify the incorrect decisions. In fact, organizations that expect near perfect decisions or that are overly critical of bad decisions typically have ineffective cultures. Ultimately, expecting perfection or being overly critical creates hesitancy on the part of the organization about its ability to make decisions and slows down progress tremendously.

TIP

The program culture that does not criticize bad decisions but chooses to learn from them and encourages participants to continue to be aggressive is usually much more productive. I once heard a program manager say, "I tell my project managers that if they make three of four decisions correctly, they are performing well. We must always reexamine our decisions, because one of four may be incorrect. When we find it quickly, we can turn it around with minimum impact. I certainly don't want people to be waiting around for perfection. Waiting for perfection causes more bad circumstances and delays than the imperfection of bad decisions."

Mentoring

Few companies do not recognize mentoring as a valuable organizational capability. However, rarely do organizations have an established process in place to ensure that mentoring occurs. Mentoring requires more than lip service; it requires a process. Who are you mentoring? Who are your project managers mentoring? Who are your technical gurus and business process experts mentoring? More important, what formalizes these relationships in the organization? Are they part of performance plans? Do targets or metrics exists for the amount of time spent mentoring? Do mentors and the people they are mentoring fill out an evaluation form assessing the effectiveness of the mentoring relationship? Does your organization recognize the positive impact made by some mentors by having a mentor of the month, quarter, or year award? The bottom line is, do you have an ingrained culture that facilitates mentoring?

I'm often amazed at how some organizations ignore mentoring and its associated professional development activities, and then wonder why they have no one available internally to fill a key vacant position or no one they can effectively divide or delegate work to. The CFO of a leading organization once told me that for every key position in their organization, they had two people identified and prepared—or preparing to—fill it. They had to have two because their competitors knew the capabilities of their personnel and routinely tried to hire them away, and sometimes their competitors were successful. The fact that they spent the resources to develop people for future opportunities was a significant component of their very low turnover rates and their ability to attract the best and brightest talent.

Long-term program success is dependent upon the continued growth and development of program personnel. Technical challenges and business complexity continue to grow. Therefore, it is only natural that the capabilities of our personnel must continue to grow also if we plan to continually outpace the competition.

SCENARIO

If you saw the movie *Apollo 13*, the flight director with the vest, who is famous for the statement "Failure is not an option" was Gene Kranz. Gene Kranz was director of Mission Operations when I hired on with NASA in Mission Operations. He regularly briefed groups of new hires that were in his organization to instill in them his expectations and perspectives, and to provide a sense of the history and culture of the organization. One of his expectations was for us to argue and debate with each other. He was concerned that young people at that time (in the early 1980s) did not like to argue and debate, but instead had a "go along and get along" mentality. He stated that we would not achieve our goals without healthy argument and debate. The briefing Gene Kranz provided was part of an overall one-year development plan for new hires that culminated with a personal briefing from the new hire to him about their first year's accomplishments in the organization.

Consider the following three points from this story.

1. He took the time to personally come and brief new employees that were at the lowest level in a very large organization.
2. A passion for constructive argument and debate is a sign of a strong organization, and traits like this, which may be seen as "countercultural" by some, have to be instilled and encouraged.

3. The fact that new hires had to come back to him in a year with their accomplishments not only encouraged outstanding work, but also helped him and the organization identify exceptional performers early.

All of these actions had nothing to do with the day-to-day critical challenges he faced. They were leadership tactics whose purpose was to create long-term benefits for the organization.

Ultimately, all program managers have significant short- and long-term challenges. If you ignore the long-term challenges of improving project management processes and culture, the short-term challenges increase in number and intensity. Therefore, a good program manager embraces his or her role and applies leadership to address short-term challenges while concurrently and continually leading the organization down a path of process and culture improvement.

KEYSTONES
Attributes of the Effective Program Manager

1. Being a program manager requires a greater skill set and more diverse background than being a project manager.
2. The most significant difference between project manager responsibility and program manager responsibility is the requirement for the program manager to establish a culture of success.
3. Self-regulation takes time to create, but it is the ultimate definition of presence. With self-regulation, the organization acts and performs just like the program manager would want it to even if he or she is not present.
4. Leadership is based on a relationship of trust, and program managers must consistently develop and use relationship capital.
5. The ability to accomplish objectives through others is directly correlated to the strength of the relationships or the relationship capital the program manager has developed.
6. Consistency in style, management techniques, and leadership traits are important anchors for any organization and contribute to a stable work environment.

7. Effective questioning starts with being perceptive and in touch with the organization—having a feel for the organization above and beyond what charts and graphs provide.

8. As program manager you want to establish a "self-regulating" culture where your team answers your questions before you ask them.

9. Decisions should be made quickly and at the appropriate level through the establishment of clear lines of accountability and escalation processes.

10. Long-term program success is dependent on the continued growth and development of program personnel.

Stakeholder Management

Stakeholder management involves everything necessary to control relationships with all individuals the program impacts or affects in order to ensure the achievement of program objectives. One of the primary concerns for any program manager should be stakeholder management, as it is an ongoing process that is never completed. Additionally, over the life of a program the stakeholders may change—new stakeholders may be added or removed—or the role of existing stakeholders may expand or contract. The program manager must be the steadying element in this ocean of change. The program manager must mentor and coach project managers in terms of stakeholder management, since project managers are often focused on deliverables, sometimes at the expense of stakeholder relationships.

Identifying Stakeholders

To begin, the program manager needs to identify all stakeholders connected with the program and on the supporting projects. William Congreve may have said, "Hell hath no fury like a woman scorned," but program managers need to remember, "Hell hath no fury like a stakeholder scorned." Realize also that a stakeholder isn't always a person. Often an organization has to be represented, in which case the organization as a whole is the stakeholder. But even when the stakeholder is more than one person, the program manager should work to obtain single-point accountability for each stakeholding organization. Additionally, the accountable person should have the power (or be delegated the power) to make decisions in his or her stakeholder role. In this regard, smart program managers will use their influence to select stakeholder representatives that are easy to work with.

To fully identify stakeholders, use the following guidelines:

- Follow the money! Whoever is paying is definitely a stakeholder. Also, if the program produces savings or additional costs for an organization, then the organization is also a stakeholder.
- Follow the resources. Every entity that provides resources, whether internal or external, labor or facilities, and equipment, is a stakeholder. Line managers and functional managers providing resources are stakeholders.
- Follow the deliverables. Whoever is the recipient of the product or service the program is providing is a stakeholder.
- Follow the signatures. The individual who signs off on completion of the final product or service (or completed phases of the product or service) is a stakeholder. Note: This may or may not be the recipient referred to in the previous bullet. Often there may be more recipients than signatories.

- Examine other programs' stakeholder lists. Include active programs and completed projects.
- Review the organizational chart to assess which parts of the organization may be stakeholders.
- Ask team members, customers, and any other confirmed stakeholder to help you identify additional stakeholders.
- Look for the "Unofficial People of Influence." These may be people who are trusted by high-level leaders or who wield a lot of power through influence and not position.

The goal of following these guidelines is to make sure every possible stakeholder is identified. Some of your stakeholders may play major roles, while others may have minor roles and little or no interest or interaction. Regardless of size or role, every stakeholder's needs must be assessed, and you cannot meet the needs of a stakeholder you have not identified. As a program manager, you must ensure that every project manager supporting the program has identified all the stakeholders for his or her project, and that the project managers are aware of the stakeholders that exist at the program level.

The program-level view is important for stakeholder management, because often several project managers may be sharing several stakeholders. In such cases, everyone needs to apply sound, strategic judgment, as you do not want to burden or overwhelm stakeholders by having them deal with multiple project managers. To avoid headaches, decide at the program level whether you need to assign a lead person to be the stakeholders' main point of contact. In some cases this contact person may be the program manager, and in other cases it may be the project manager who has the predominant workload with that stakeholder. Or it may be the project manager who has previously established a good rapport and strong relationship with the stakeholder.

Whoever it is, the program should speak with a single voice so that in cases where stakeholders must deal with multiple program representatives, program coordination takes place prior to stakeholder coordination.

Know Your Stakeholders' *Pets*

Pet peeves . . . pet projects . . . pet people: Every stakeholder usually has one or more of these. Your job is to know what or who they are. You can uncover this information through observation, organizational research, or asking stakeholders directly (if your relationship is strong enough). Find out what your stakeholders' biggest pains and worries are. Also find out how their performance is judged. After all, people behave according to how they are rewarded. When you determine how they are rewarded, then you can predict behavior. Knowing what motivates your stakeholder is important. So ask yourself, "What makes the stakeholder's customer or boss say the equivalent of "good job" to the stakeholder?

Assess the Stakeholders' Power

Once you have identified all the stakeholders, you need to analyze their potential impact on the program. This includes assessing each stakeholder's power. You should know the limits of their power, as well as how much they can hurt you and how much they can help you. Assess their history of using that power. Knowing what has caused them to exercise power in the past is very valuable, as it is usually a predictor of what will or can cause them to exercise their power in the future. You'll also find that many stakeholders have power but never use it. This information enables you to know how to gain access to that power in case you need it later. Finally, you should know what type of power each stakeholder has. Is it positional, influence, expert, charismatic, etc.?

A common method of analyzing stakeholders is to plot their level of power and preference. In Figure 3.1, the following definitions apply:

- *High*—The stakeholder has the power to kill the project or keep the project viable when under attack.
- *Medium*—The stakeholder has the power to help/impede the project's process or to partner with and influence other stakeholders to keep/kill the project.
- *Low*—The stakeholder has little or no influence to help/impede the project.
- *For*—The stakeholder fully supports the project.
- *Indifferent*—The stakeholder is uninformed or indifferent about the project.
- *Against*—The stakeholder is against the project.

FIGURE 3.1 Stakeholder Assessment

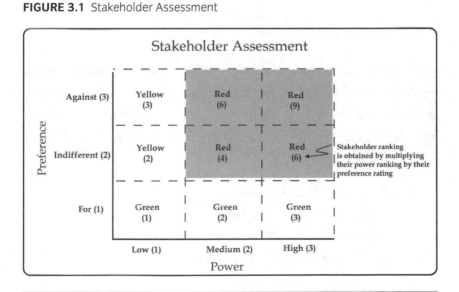

Calculate the score by multiplying the stakeholders' power by their preference. Any score of 4 or above requires proactive work with the stakeholder, and the program manager should ensure contingency plans are in place in case of adverse stakeholder action. This method attempts to identify the powerful stakeholders who are against and who are for the program and its projects. This method can provide value, but its simplicity, compared with the complexity of stakeholder relationships and organizational culture, makes its use at face value very risky.

The stakeholder assessment grid is a static representation, and as business conditions and the organization changes over time, so can stakeholder preferences. Programs are also complex, so while this grid may work well for individual projects, stakeholders may have varying preferences for projects and initiatives within a program. This tool is a good one but is more applicable at the project level. If used at the program level, individual projects should be delineated. In any case, understand the "why" of stakeholder preferences and always pay attention to powerful stakeholders, whether they are for or against the program.

The Problem Stakeholder

Chances are high that you will at some point have one or a few problem stakeholders in the mix. This comes with the territory, and is a challenge you must overcome to maximize your program's success. Problem stakeholders come in a variety of flavors, including the following:

- The meddling stakeholder
- The overbearing stakeholder
- The poor stakeholder
- The untrustworthy stakeholder
- The indecisive stakeholder
- The unavailable stakeholder

I hope you never have a meddling, overbearing, poor, untrustworthy, indecisive stakeholder who is never available. In most cases, once the problem stakeholder surfaces, your best defense is to face the problem head on and meet with the individual stakeholder to resolve the issue. First, let's address how to deal with each of the stakeholder types mentioned.

The Meddling Stakeholder. The meddling stakeholder is always inserting himself or herself into decisions, processes, or meetings where his or her presence is not required. As a program manager, you must protect your project managers from the meddling stakeholder. Even better, coach your project managers to develop "rules of engagement" for dealing with all stakeholders, including meddling ones.

Before discussing the matter with the meddling stakeholder, the program and project managers should assess the cause of the stakeholder meddling and listen to the meddling stakeholder to ascertain whether his or her experience may help in any way. Assess, strategize, and then engage.

Some stakeholders meddle because they lack a relationship of trust with the project manager. Causes for the lack of trust can include:

- The stakeholder doesn't trust the project manager's ability.
- The stakeholder was just burned on a previous project.
- The stakeholder has a historical distrust for your organization based on previous failures or reputation.

Overcoming a lack of trust can be difficult, especially if it is justified by previous performance. Building trust begins with communication and demonstrated competence. Expect trust building to take time. In the meantime, acknowledge the lack of trust and state that you plan to regain the stakeholder's trust.

Other times stakeholders meddle because they are control freaks. Sometimes these control freak stakeholders are so busy meddling that they neglect their own responsibilities and duties. Finally, a small percentage of meddling stakeholders are really "last-job"-holding stakeholders. That is, this stakeholder finds the transition to his or her new, higher-level position uncomfortable for whatever reason and still wants to "dabble" in "old" responsibilities as much as possible.

The program manager must ensure that project managers aren't hampered by the meddling stakeholder by making sure that certain rules of engagement are established and enforced as to when stakeholder involvement is necessary. "Enforced" is a strong word here, and and usually whatever enforcement is required should be done diplomatically. These rules of engagement may be written or verbal. If verbal, it is prudent for the program manager to ensure project managers document them as appropriate. Rules of engagement not only help control meddling stakeholders; they can also foster better relationships with all stakeholders. Having standardized rules for dealing with stakeholders within a program is good, but you'll typically need to tailor the rules for each project.

One of the most critical stakeholder rules of engagement concerns how often and what format routine communication with the stakeholder will take place. For the high-level or high-powered stakeholders, I recommend "face-to-face" or telephone communication be established as a mandatory part of the routine communication processes. Always try not to deliver documents via e-mail or fax without some kind of verbal explanation ahead of time. Chances are the stakeholders will not be able to properly interpret results of reports, especially if they're not given the opportunity to verbally ask questions. Many times stakeholders harbor concerns or uneasiness that could be quickly addressed with verbal communication. This kind of communication can be handled with regularly scheduled meetings if the stakeholder attends. If not, the project manager and/or program manager should phone the stakeholder weekly or whenever necessary depending upon the circumstances. Even if the stakeholder is unavailable, leaving a message describing any major decisions or issues (or even if you state there are no issues and everything is proceeding as planned for the week) goes a long way toward building confidence.

Another strategy for dealing with the meddling stakeholder is to overwhelm them with tasks and communication. They insist on being involved, so involve them. If the stakeholder has time to be this involved, give them work to do and assign actions to keep them busy with nonrisky or unimportant activities. Real work often makes people invisible, and may make the meddling stakeholder invisible too.

The Overbearing Stakeholder. An overbearing stakeholder, because of his or her power position or personality, can be domineering and put the program at risk. Take care to minimize the damage these people can do to a program. Often, the program manager will have to step in to defend and insulate project managers from overbearing stakeholders. Additionally, program managers should ensure that the overbearing stakeholder cannot spoil or ruin customer relationships and other important relationships. This is why, although on the surface it may seem logical to have meetings with all stakeholders together, sometimes it is more prudent to meet with stakeholders individually to minimize unnecessary conflict or grandstanding. As a program manager, you must assess and plan a strategy for stakeholder interaction. Often, the program manager serves as the go-between for stakeholders and project managers, in order to foster positive relationships and provide the project managers with the maximum opportunity for success.

The Poor Stakeholder. A poor stakeholder is someone who has interests in or is impacted by the program, but who has no significant budget or budget authority. Thus, they are usually at a power disadvantage as compared with other stakeholders. As such, they may play politics in order to gain influence to protect their position or achieve their objectives. The program manager must take care not to ignore the poor stakeholder; otherwise, he or she could become a roadblock. Understanding of how the objectives of the poor stakeholder line up or conflict with those of the more powerful stakeholders is very important, because it can be a predictor of how they will behave concerning future issues.

The Untrustworthy Stakeholder. The untrustworthy stakeholder will often play "both sides," won't stand by his or her words, and will refuse to document anything with a signature. No magic bullet exists for how to deal with untrustworthy stakeholders. Fear of accountability, inexperience, and/or ignorance can contribute to untrustworthiness. Even worse is when the person is intentionally untrustworthy. When it comes to dealing with an untrustworthy stakeholder, the program manager should ensure that all important communication relative to the program and projects within the program are documented and have traceability. If possible, the program manager should work to remove or disempower untrustworthy stakeholders.

Untrustworthy people are one of the most devastating forces that can hinder a program or organization's effectiveness. Therefore, deploy short-term tactics and longer-term strategies to eliminate untrustworthy stakeholders, even if it is a three- to five-year plan with clandestine tactics. This means keeping a history with data (examples of events and impacts) of untrustworthy behavior or circumstances and patiently waiting for the right set of circumstances in which to use the data to take proactive action to neutralize the stakeholder. This may involve partnering with others who are also impacted by the untrustworthy behavior. Proceed with caution, but do proceed. It is unusual for the genuinely untrustworthy person to one day wake up trustworthy.

People at all levels who can be proven untrustworthy should be helped to a happier place, meaning to where they have no role or influence on the program any longer. Remember, kill what's ugly while it is young. Untrustworthiness is the ugliest of ugly.

The Indecisive Stakeholder. The indecisive stakeholder can never make decisions in a timely manner or cannot remain committed to previous decisions he or she has made. Few traits are more debilitating to the organization than indecision. When dealing with the indecisive stakeholder you must set up processes and structures that clearly communicate when the decision is required and the impact of the decision not being made. Set a definite date for when a decision is due and identify upfront the consequences of not making the decision on time. Keep a log of these consequences and/or establish a metric of lost time due to delayed decisions. This also applies to high-level stakeholders, who should not be given a free ride because of their position or power base.

Many projects and programs lose a half day here, a day there, or sometimes weeks and months due to stakeholders who find a reason to wait rather than decide. Try to find out why the stakeholder is indecisive and address those reasons over the short and long term. Hopefully, indecision is not a trait that is systemic to the organization as a whole. Systemic indecision is a common problem in some organizations, especially among middle management. The program manager has to ensure that project managers are not waiting on decisions or being hampered by the indecisiveness of the organization. The incompetence of indecision must be exposed privately and politely at first, and then strategically migrated to publicly and painfully . . . if that is what it takes to eliminate the incompetence.

The Unavailable Stakeholder. The unavailable stakeholder is always "too busy" to participate when their input or approval is required. Handle the unavailable stakeholder with care. It is often the unavailable stakeholder who ends up questioning or challenging the program and project deliverables at pivotal points when they had prior opportunities to review and provide input.

Strategies for dealing with the unavailable stakeholder include:

1. Trying to get the stakeholder to delegate authority to someone capable and trustworthy who will be available.
2. Working with the stakeholder to provide a mechanism to allow the stakeholder to make decisions without having to be physically present.
3. Having project managers determine the best available times for all stakeholders at the beginning of the project and/or establish meeting dates or a plan as to how ad hoc meetings will be scheduled and get stakeholder agreement on this. Ad hoc meetings may be appropriate instead of regularly scheduled meetings, depending upon the circumstances.
4. Maintaining scheduled meetings and timeframes to avoid the cycle of continually rescheduling meetings, as this can contribute to stakeholders becoming unavailable.
5. Publishing stakeholder meeting schedules well in advance and following up with telephone and e-mail reminders.
6. Accessing the stakeholder at opportunistic times, like lunch breaks, social events, their walk into and out of the building, etc.

The program manager should require project managers to maintain a record of all attempts made to communicate with the unavailable stakeholder. As this record takes shape, the program manager will have acquired data to use when requesting the stakeholder either to change his or her behavior or to delegate or resign from his or her stakeholder responsibilities.

Above all else, you need to deal aggressively with problem stakeholders. As a program manager, your role is to clear the way for project managers by dealing with problem stakeholders directly or making sure the project managers have a valid and viable strategy for managing the stakeholder. The program manager should always question the project managers to ensure there are thorough and well-thought-out plans in place for dealing with the problem stakeholders.

The Ideal Stakeholder

The following points highlight the attributes of the ideal stakeholder.

1. Shows an interest in the project or program
2. Makes himself/herself available when necessary
3. Assigns qualified personnel to act on the stakeholder's behalf when the stakeholder is unavailable
4. Has a willingness to be accountable. Reviews and signs required documents in a timely manner
5. Tells the program or project managers his communication preferences
6. Prioritizes her preferences and requirements
7. Understands the project management process and does not pressure project managers to circumvent it
8. Looks for opportunities to provide relief to program personnel as appropriate
9. Helps motivate program personnel and shows appreciation for good work

Build Relationships with the Stakeholders

Relationship building with stakeholders is one of the most important aspects of program management. Realize that relationship building never ends. Relationships can always be strengthened. Unfortunately, relationship building is something the novice or technically focused program managers often overlook. They are so focused on the tangible deliverables of the project that they discount the importance of relationship building.

A strong stakeholder relationship begins by establishing trust and then continually building on that trust. Ultimately you want to treat the stakeholder like he or she wants to be treated. This means taking time to find out about the stakeholder. The more you know about the stakeholder, the easier it will be to engage him or her in positive conversation about the program.

The most effective sales personnel know their customer best. It usually pays dividends to invest time learning the personal and professional history of stakeholders. Discretely gathering information on stakeholder preferences may seem "out of the box" for some, but most major service providers of all types and levels make it a practice to collect information on their best customers. Using this information makes it easy to establish strong rapport with stakeholders. It also makes it easier to handle situations that arise when new project managers come on board, because you can quickly brief the new managers about the stakeholders and identify areas of common interest and common ground.

Building rapport like this is vital, because you want to have trust firmly established before you have the intense pressures of program dilemmas and decisions to work through.

Additionally, you need to keep your stakeholders' "keepers" and support personnel happy. Therefore, foster and develop relationships with the secretary and the staff of high-level stakeholders. It does not take a rocket scientist to figure out that if the high-level stakeholder's secretary likes you, then you are more likely to have access to the high-level stakeholder.

You should also foster a relationship between your stakeholders and the person who backs you up or acts on your behalf when you are unavailable. For a variety of reasons you may be unavailable to personally respond to every stakeholder request, and you should have someone else at the ready in whom stakeholders have confidence.

Relationships with remote stakeholders entail many barriers to building a strong relationship of trust. Such relationships often experience communication barriers, culture barriers, time difference obstacles, as well as the natural impediments that exist when human beings cannot communicate face-to-face. If the stakeholder relationship is important, it pays to make arrangements to travel and meet face-to-face.

Barring face-to-face communication opportunities, communication by telephone is very important. Just as there is no magic bullet for remote relationship building, there is no substitute for face-to-face communication. Expect more risk with remote stakeholders, especially if a lack of travel funds or busy schedules prevents face-to-face relationship building because the relationships will not be as strong and communication (especially informal) is more challenging. I am aware of one global company that outsources some project management work to India, but only after the remote project managers have spent six weeks in the United States getting to know project managers and team members.

Build Relationships among Stakeholders

Program managers benefit when the relationships among the stakeholders are strong. Strong relationships minimize political grandstanding and usually facilitate compromises and/or solutions that are best for the organization and are not always in a specific stakeholder's self-interest. So in addition to creating strong relationships between the program management team and the stakeholders, the program manager should foster positive relationships among stakeholders. The first step in this process is to always be positive and speak positively about all stakeholders. Don't get baited or caught in the trap of talking negatively about a particular stakeholder whether that party deserves it or not.

TIP

Whenever the stakeholders are together, take some time to introduce them formally and informally. Share some positive or unique attribute about each stakeholder. I first saw this done by Robert "Bob" Crippen, who was the pilot on the first Space Shuttle mission and who held numerous leadership roles within NASA, when he was chairing a conference. He had a kind word and career highlight for every person he introduced. In this way, Bob built bridges between the conference attendees and the speakers, who were high-level program stakeholders. He effectively warmed the audience by relaxing both the speaker and those in the audience. This made the speaker more approachable for one-on-one conversations during scheduled interaction times.

If you have done your homework, developing a relationship with each stakeholder like this should not be difficult. You can also start a meeting with an appropriate ice-breaking activity. Appropriate means it fits the group of stakeholders. For example, do they all know each other? Have they worked together for years? Is someone new to the group? In the case where you have one or a few stakeholders new to an existing group, take the time to make personal introductions of the new stakeholders. You can also send existing members a note about the new stakeholder's background and interests he or she may have in common with others in the group, and encourage them to make the new stakeholder(s) feel welcome.

Start early developing positive relationships among stakeholders, because pressure tends to increase with program longevity and as project delivery dates approach. When scheduling meetings with stakeholders, allocate additional time for breaks or schedule the meeting over lunch or breakfast to create a relaxed atmosphere that fosters relationship development.

Be careful about jumping into conflicts among high-powered stakeholders. Often their conflicts are much deeper and longer-lived than they appear on the surface. Even though your role as the program manager includes fostering strong relationships among stakeholders, there will always be a few relationships whose repair or improvement is beyond your scope and ability. Therefore, use trusted resources to find out about and keep up with the status of the relationships among stakeholders . . . and know when not to interfere.

Realize that relationship building does not overcome incompetence. Your credibility as a program manager and your project managers' credibility are necessary elements for strong relationships with project stakeholders. Expect stakeholders to check up on you and your project managers, especially if the relationships are new and/or the service or deliverable the program provides is critical. Anticipate stakeholder needs and questions. Contact them quickly, in person or by phone, for critical information they should know.

SCENARIO

A Space Shuttle program manager once told me he learned not to wait on the "system" to relay important information to important stakeholders. He further stated that when the information did get to the stakeholder in a timely manner, it was often biased, out of context, or didn't tell the complete story. Therefore, after important meetings he would personally call all major stakeholders that weren't present to advise them of the discussion and the outcome. This also provided him the opportunity to field questions and listen to concerns. Over time this built strong relationships of trust.

Always be prepared for presentations and meetings. Ensure that your team is prepared as well. Teach your project managers that when they don't know an answer to a question a stakeholder is asking, they need to say, "I don't know, but I will find out by [a specific time and date]." Project managers should know that stakeholders often ask questions they already know the answer to, or to which they know there is no answer. They are simply testing the presenter's credibility.

Communication Strategies for Stakeholders

Effective communication builds and establishes trust. While consistency in communication with stakeholders is the goal, it is equally important to meet with each stakeholder and find out what are his or her communications needs. Also, you need to identify how each stakeholder may want "special" communication (face-to-face or by telephone). With high-level stakeholders you should also identify whom they want you to communicate with in the event they are unavailable. Define for the stakeholder ahead of time the criteria for "special" communication. Program or project emergencies and items of political significance may warrant special communication with the customer.

Take care to avoid or minimize "specialized" regular briefings of stakeholders that are outside of the regular communication process in order to minimize duplication of effort or to imply favoritism. Therefore, prearrangement on report structure, frequency, and format at the beginning of the stakeholder relationship is advantageous. The program manager should strive for a common structure for all stakeholders and avoid providing stakeholders too much detail.

Milestones are important communication opportunities for dealing with stakeholders. The program manager should actually start communicating the status to the stakeholder well before the milestone. The goal of the precommunication is to eliminate any possibility the stakeholder will be surprised by something at the milestone review, and that he or she is adequately prepared for the review and the sign-off of any deliverables associated with the milestone.

Following are some actual communication techniques that will help when delivering information:

- *Whispering*—It is always appropriate to whisper bad news or significant information to the stakeholder. By "whispering" I mean communicating to the stakeholder the needed information under casual circumstances existing before the information is publicly or widely known. Whispering means you intentionally "bump into" the stakeholder somewhere. To do this effectively, you need to know the stakeholder's habits and/or schedule. Knowing where stakeholders park, as well as their arrival and departure times, always served me well with many opportunities to casually bump into a stakeholder. Whispering also is very important when you need to prepare stakeholders for a negative risk event that may happen. Letting them know ahead of time of the potential event, your plans to prevent the event, and how you will deal with the event's consequences should it occur minimizes any negative reaction and/or response when the event actually occurs. When stakeholders accept or add to your plan for the risk event, it becomes a shared risk—one that minimizes the likelihood of stakeholder overreaction if the risk event materializes. Additionally, a shared risk establishes a positive framework for development and/or execution of the contingency plan to deal with the materialized risk.
- *Cheat Sheets*—High-level stakeholders may manage a multitude of tasks and issues concurrently. As such, it is often difficult for them, or any other human for that matter, to keep abreast of every activity. To make it easy on them, provide a "cheat sheet" before major meetings. After you provide this a few times you will find they will start to ask you for it. On the cheat sheet, include bulleted, succinct information about major issues, including any questions

they should ask at the meeting and the anticipated outcome and/or purpose of the meeting. This cheat sheet
typically should be no more than half to three-quarters of
a page long, and will be something that rapidly brings
them up to speed on key items. Cheat sheets are a means
of providing condensed and concise information to stakeholders throughout the life of the program, thus minimizing a lot of issues that often arise from miscommunication
and speculation.

Lead the Stakeholders

We began this chapter with the quote "Hell hath no fury like a
stakeholder scorned." Here is an example of how true that statement is. One multimillion-dollar project I am aware of was near-
ing completion and was in fact ready to be implemented. The
project was complex. The only thing that prevented implementation was the approval of the highest-level stakeholder, who had
been advised against the implementation by another stakeholder,
one who really didn't understand what had to be done. Although
the program manager and project managers had done a good job
of creating the project deliverables, they had not effectively understood and addressed the concerns of all stakeholders. And in fact,
this particular stakeholder's concerns could have been easily
addressed had the program manager been paying attention. In the
end, the high-level stakeholder, who felt ignored, essentially terminated the project.

You also need to educate stakeholders on the project management processes that you and your team will be deploying, as well as
the role each stakeholder may or may not play in those processes.
Creating buy-in on the project management processes with stakeholders makes it easier to maintain the discipline necessary to

follow these processes. That's why the program manager has to manage his or her stakeholders at the program level and make sure project managers are managing their stakeholders. Often the stakeholders may be the same, and the program manager has to determine whether stakeholder management can and should be delegated to the project manager. Even if delegation cannot be fully done, the program manager is often well served by delegating portions of stakeholder management to project managers.

The program manager has to lead the stakeholders, even when they are much more powerful and/or higher in the organization's structure. This is also true of project managers, and the program manager needs to clearly communicate this requirement to all project managers. Both program and project managers need to champion and lead their project and not be intimidated by a stakeholder's position or authority.

Program managers should also check up on how well project managers are doing stakeholder management by periodically (weekly or monthly or at milestones) calling the stakeholder and asking how the project manager is doing and whether their needs are being met. The program manager should inform project managers from the beginning that this quality check will take place. Never assume that no news is good news when dealing with stakeholders.

When program milestones are completed or when there is a change in stakeholders, the program manager should take the time to thank stakeholders for their contribution. Recognizing stakeholders' contributions helps them feel like they are a part of the team and are likely to generate more "team" behavior than "us versus them" behavior.

Stakeholder management is an ongoing process that requires time and proper execution. Unfortunately, project managers and project teams, for a variety of reasons, often do not spend adequate time and effort on stakeholder management. Thus, stakeholder management must be a point of focus for the program manager, who has to assure execution of strategically planned processes to maintain positive and valuable stakeholder relationships.

Stakeholder Management

1. Stakeholder management involves everything necessary to control relationships with all individuals the program impacts or affects in order to ensure the achievement of program objectives.
2. Program managers must mentor and coach project managers in terms of stakeholder management.
3. Program managers need to make certain that all stakeholders for the program and on supporting projects are identified.
4. Know your stakeholder's pet peeves . . . pet projects . . . pet people.
5. There will always be a few problem stakeholders and they must be handled to allow project manager and program success.
6. Relationship building with stakeholders is one of the most important aspects of program management and never ends.
7. Program managers have to foster strong relationships among stakeholders.
8. Stakeholders' communication needs should be assessed, agreed upon, and made as uniformly consistent as possible.
9. The program manager has to lead the stakeholders and teach project managers to lead stakeholders, even when the stakeholders are much more powerful.

Program Process Strategy

A good part of the program manager's strategy is to
develop the program's culture. Very often, all of the elements that
affect program culture are not under the program manager's direct
control. Many times, the program manager must work with these
"outside elements" to assure a positive program culture.

For example, deciding which processes to use to conduct project management is a strategic program decision. If the organization has a project management office (PMO) that establishes
project management processes, the PMO has a direct impact on
program culture. This means the program manager must work
with the PMO to assure that the processes are having a positive
impact on his or her program. The same is true for human
resources, procurement, and other service providers and process
creators in the organization.

Often, things that negatively affect one program manager also negatively impact other program managers in the organization, and it may be productive for program managers to strategically band together to drive positive change. People and projects will come and go, but the program culture will remain and needs to be managed in such a way that it not only allows project managers to be successful, but in fact makes it difficult for them to fail.

Creating Program Culture

If you had to teach a hundred nonswimmers to swim, you could line them up at the edge of a pool, throw them in the water, and say, "Swim!" A small percentage would swim and be successful without instruction. The majority, however, would have to be pulled from the pool to avoid disaster. But with a proper culture—in this case, proper instruction—all one hundred swimmers could learn effectively.

Similarly, some in your organization already know how to succeed and how to deliver projects regardless of the culture they work in. You'll find that a small percentage of project managers can and always will deliver the goods, regardless of the circumstances. Often their success can lead us to believe incorrectly that those who are not as successful are somehow less capable or are deficient. But, as leaders, we have to create a culture that maximizes the success and development of all project managers, not just the gifted few who seem able to do well with or without us.

To extend the swimming analogy for a minute, if we were teaching swimmers, we would care about the temperature, depth, and condition of the water. As our students' skill level progressed, we would hold classes in swimming in a strong current, pounding ocean surf, or a swollen river. Even those who swim at the highest levels of competition have a coach and a structured regimen they follow in order to continually improve.

How cold is the "water" for your project managers? How deep is it? Is it crystal clear, or cloudy and green with algae? How many obstacles must they fight through in order to "swim"? How good a "coach" is your organization? Do those on your team have a structured regimen that helps them improve to their maximum potential? Is there a "lifeguard" on duty to help them out of tough situations? Do they have a partner to ensure that neither gets lost or in trouble? Do you have a sink or swim, "every project manager for themselves" culture, or an "everyone here can be a strong swimmer" culture?

As a leader, you must assess the culture you create for your project managers and implement changes that are not just quick fixes of single problems, but have positive long-term effects on the culture. Though earned value can be an effective project management tool, an organization must have a mature enough project management culture to implement it. Earned value is of little use if you do not have relatively stable schedules and up-to-date, relevant cost information.

Analyze your project management culture. Ask your project managers what one thing about the way the organization conducts project management they would change if they could. Pay attention to what they say, and listen to your instincts about which of the suggested improvements you could implement. You are likely to find that you have more improvement opportunities than you can effectively implement right away; therefore, prioritize them and make the top items a reality for your project managers.

Changing culture takes time, continued action, follow-up, and communication. Identifying a solution may be easy, but the challenge lies in implementing and instilling that solution within the organization. If it were easy, every organization would have a great, highly effective culture. Therefore, you must grow accustomed to deferring gratification when it comes to changing culture, even as you maintain passions and initiate actions to change it.

When a mistake happens or a project fails, a few people will criticize the individual perceived to be responsible. However, the more perceptive leaders will ask an important question, which I have learned to ask myself and which I challenge you to ask when something goes amiss: "How did we, as management, set this person up to fail? We know the person is capable and has a desire to do the right thing and be successful, so what is it about our process and our culture that caused him or her to fail?"

When you ask and answer this question, you are on your way to creating and improving a culture of success. Remember, it is often your best people that make the worst mistakes, because your best people do the most complex work. For this reason, they will try to do what it takes to make it happen and will try the most creative solutions. The average worker is not only doing less work, but he or she is also doing less risky work and is less likely to make mistakes. Teach your project managers and regulate yourself not to overreact when people make mistakes. Culture change takes time, but the investment is worth the effort.

Balancing Program Process Objectives

"Now wait a minute," the program manager said. "We made a conscious decision to . . ." The program manager said these words after some unpleasant consequences from a decision had surfaced. While the consequences were unpleasant, they were not unexpected, and this was the program manager's point. Almost every course of action a leader takes comes with or has the potential for a certain degree of unpleasantness. The perfect solution without negative ramifications may exist at the end of the rainbow, but in the real world, decisions and solutions aren't perfect and usually involve some kind of negative consequence to bear in order to gain the positive benefits.

Program managers are required to pick the organization's pain and shortcomings. To do so, the program manager has to strike balances between opposing objectives. Realize that the decision that establishes the point of balance will never be perfect, because programs and organizations are fluid, but perfect is not a requirement for success. Rather, the requirement for success is to strike the point of balance while understanding the positive and negative ramifications of that balance point. Proper adjustment to these points of balance as conditions dictate is essential for continued success. Accepting and accounting for the negative ramifications associated with the chosen balance point is what I mean by "picking your pain."

Consider the following opposing objectives:

- People dependency versus process dependency
- Time spent planning versus time spent executing
- Resources spent on new projects versus resources spent on maintenance
- Resources spent on research versus resources spent on operations
- Time spent training versus time spent performing work activities

The amount of time or resources spent on one of these objectives eliminates the amount of time or resources spent on the opposing objective. For example, when I am training project managers or project team members, they are not performing their project management duties. I am aware of organizations that provide project managers two to three weeks of training per year, while others provide zero training opportunities for their project managers (they're too busy chopping to stop and sharpen the axe).

Each end of this example includes pain and shortcomings. The organization that provides two to three weeks of training per year has to plan for and deal with the consequences of having their project teams absent during that time. This absence could have a negative impact on the project and possibly on relationships with stakeholders. The organization that provides zero training for its project managers has to deal with project managers who are improving at a slower rate than project managers who are receiving training. Additionally, employees who do not receive training often feel less valued by the organization, and thus the turnover rate for these employees is usually higher. This then impacts recruiting, as most high-achieving job candidates are interested in personal and professional growth. The organization that provides zero training is communicating to its employees "your growth is not important to us." So while zero training may be best for short-term program objectives, three weeks of training may be best for long-term program health and capability growth. The program manager must strategically choose the balance point.

Pain will happen. Shortcomings will definitely occur. The question is, does your organization and program choose the pain and shortcomings, or do they just happen haphazardly? In our example, choosing would mean making a commitment to three weeks of training per year and having the discipline to maintain the commitment. Haphazard is when a program manager says, "We would like to provide training as soon as things slow down." The result is that two years later, little or no training has occurred.

The American Heritage Dictionary of the English Language defines *haphazard* as "dependent upon or characterized by mere chance." Unfortunately, a lot of programs are led this way. Specifically, the program manager does not make conscious decisions relative to key elements of program strategy, thus causing haphazard results. The dictionary defines "conscious" as "Intentionally conceived or done; deliberate" and "Having an awareness of one's environment and one's own existence, sensations, and thoughts."

Execute Process Strategy Keys

It is easy for program managers to get consumed with the "urgent" and the "tactical." However, at the program level, you also need to devote significant time to the "strategic." That is, every program manager has to develop strategies for the business growth and health of his or her program. The strategies we are discussing are for the program's internal stability and strength. The decisions that follow the strategies should not be characterized by mere chance. These decisions include:

1. How status will be performed
2. How mentoring relationships will be established
3. How project managers are assigned
4. How strategies are designed to ensure organizational discipline
5. How to mix project management responsibilities with organizational responsibilities
6. How to determine the percentage of organizational resources to spend on operations/maintenance versus development
7. How project management administrative functions are assigned
8. How to grow organizational capabilities by increasing the capabilities of project managers
9. How to balance process and people

Let's look at each in more detail.

How Status Will Be Performed

Inside a program there are thousands of tasks, issues, action items, and risks. The goal of the status process is to make the program personnel who need to be aware of something aware of it with a minimum of overhead. Realize that status is a process. The status process shouldn't be something everyone has to figure out, and there should not be significant variation in how the status is performed across the program. The status process should contribute to a stable culture. A consistent and effective status process is the keystone of a stable program culture and should help project managers be successful.

The status process should expose problems and decision opportunities. It should be partnered throughout the program, both internally and externally. The status process should be thought out and periodically monitored. Like any process, it needs to have a process owner. While the process owner is typically the program manager, this is something you can delegate to one of the program's project managers. People should know how to change the process, and the process owner manages these changes as appropriate.

The process owner needs to review the status process annually for improvement opportunities. The rapid improvement of technology and naturally occurring organizational change can cause the status process to lose its effectiveness over time. Additionally, like any other process, it must be continually evaluated for creeping bureaucracy and people violating or not conforming to the process. (Detailed recommendations for the status process will be provided in Chapter 5.)

How Mentoring Relationships Will Be Established

Mentoring is a process that requires a conscious decision on the part of the program manager and should not be left to chance. Mentoring works well when appropriately tied to the evaluation system or performance goals for project managers. If people are not being assessed, graded, or rewarded for mentoring, you cannot expect mentoring to occur. Therefore, establish mentoring agreements. The astute program manager knows who is mentoring each one of his or her project managers and key staff personnel.

Clearly define the relationship agreement between the mentor and the mentee. People often mistakenly assume the mentor serves as the advisor for everything. While there is nothing inherently wrong with this assumption, often people need mentors (and people can serve as mentors) for very specific purposes only. For example, a senior project manager may serve as a mentor for managing risks to several junior-level project managers. Their mentoring relationship may or may not include more than this, but the topic of managing risks is defined in their mentoring agreement. Conversely, a junior-level or new project manager may serve as the mentor for a senior project manager on Microsoft Access. The point here is that no one is perfect and everyone should have the opportunity to learn from others.

It is up to the program manager to jump-start and facilitate the mentoring process. You maximize the mentoring relationship when you have a mentoring process in place and give it some focus. Be sure that all mentors are rewarded and recognized. This does not have to be public, big, or fancy. A simple "thank you" and acknowledgment that the program manager is paying attention to mentoring goes a long way. Some large organizations even establish a "mentor of the year" award to let everyone know that the organization values mentoring. Whenever you are documenting performance, writing award nominations, or justifying a promotion, include a sentence or two on the mentoring the individual has accomplished to reinforce this behavior.

Mentoring relationships can cross organizational boundaries, and the program manager does not have to limit his or her selection of mentors to the program if wider opportunities are available. If the organization has several program managers, establish agreements to have other program managers mentor your project managers, and you, in turn, mentor one or more of theirs.

Realize that all mentoring doesn't have to be done in person, and you can garner some effective results by other means. For example, the program manager can have quarterly book reviews, where a leadership or other relevant book is issued to each project manager. At the end of the quarter, the entire team meets to assess the book. The assessment can require each team member to pick the three most important "take-aways" from the book, and/or have a rotating schedule that allows one or two project managers present at each meeting a summary of the good points from the book and what they or the program should consider adopting. Add some pizza or bagels to the meeting and you have an instant team-building activity that adds value.

Mentoring fosters teamwork through more and stronger relationship bonds being established. The consequences of not having a strategy for mentoring are significant, and include the slow growth—or lack of any growth—of organizational capability. The experienced program manager knows that the answer is not always more people, but rather it is more capable people. Mentoring increases the capability of the entire program. I have come across many organizations that, when they lose a key project manager, say, "We have no one capable or ready to replace him [or her]." This usually occurs because the organization is not doing anything of significance to develop the capability of their existing personnel.

How Project Managers Are Assigned

Traditionally, project managers are assigned to a project and are expected to oversee the project from beginning to end. There is nothing wrong with tradition, and this method of assigning project managers does have its advantages, such as continuity and strength of relationships with stakeholders. However, since there are other ways to assign project managers, the program manager must think strategically and pick a method that provides the program the most benefit from a short- and long-term perspective.

A powerful strategy that is often overlooked is to assign project managers by project phase. For example, in baseball, pitchers are typically categorized as starters, relievers, and closers. Starters usually have a history of very good performance and are considered more capable than relievers. Relievers are considered capable of maintaining control but typically are not as strong as a starter or a closer. Closers are often considered better than starters and their use is limited to the special situation when the game is almost over and a win is on the line.

Program managers should consider assigning project managers in the same way a baseball manager assigns pitchers. In other words, the most senior personnel can be used to kick off the project to ensure a good beginning. Once the requirements are established and baselined, a transition can occur to a more junior project manager capable of maintaining control for a project that has a good start. This transition has to be formal, with "sign-off" among the two project managers. The stakeholders must also be prepared for transition and may be included in the transition process. Once the transition is complete, the junior project manager may run the project until the project is ready to close. Then a switch can be made to a project manager who is more skilled or who specializes in closing projects.

Closing out a project is vital. The experienced program manager should recognize that the skills required to start and organize a project, (herd and manage stakeholders), are different than the skills required to manage an established project, and are different than the skills needed to close a project. Taking a project from 90 percent complete to 100 percent complete is often more challenging than taking a project from 30 percent complete to 90 percent complete. Most experienced project managers are familiar with the project timeline, where the project is 30, 60, 80, 90 percent complete, and then 96, 97, 97.5 percent complete. Often as you approach 100 percent complete, the project becomes more difficult to close for a variety of reasons, including:

- Most of the exciting work is complete and what is left is administrative in nature.
- The customer may be enjoying the benefits of project deliverables (delivery is not close-out) and this contributes to the project now becoming low priority compared with other projects.
- The customer doesn't want to close out the project because he or she wants to use it to make additional changes or to tweak the project deliverables.
- Closing-out of project contracts and/or administrative tasks wasn't properly planned for.

This phased approach to assigning projects helps the program manager maximize the use of his most highly and/or uniquely skilled project managers. Additionally, because of these different skill sets, some project managers have a natural affinity and ability for starting projects and excel at it. So a by-product of this method can be increased employee satisfaction among your most critical personnel.

You can take this method of assigning project managers a step further when outsourcing or when global operations are concerned. Depending upon the experience balance, the outsourced project manager may serve as the most experienced project manager, and he or she can start the project. Or, in the case of global operations, to ensure consistency in operations in different locations, a subset of project managers may start all projects.

This phased approach of assigning project managers can help struggling project managers. Additionally, a side benefit of assigning project managers by phase is that the organization and stakeholders learn to accept the fact that project managers will be changed. Therefore, when you have to change a project manager for another reason, the organization more readily adapts and there is less of a stigma of failure if the move was for non-performance.

Realize that this phased-approach strategy requires a strong checklist for defining what needs to be accomplished to make the project successful. However, this is not really additional work, because the transition checklist should exist anyway. After all, over a program's life, odds are very high there will be project manager changes mid-stream due to other factors.

When assigning project managers, think about and have a strategy for backing up the project manager. Frequently, when I mention "backups" in my training classes, people snicker or laugh. The bottom line is that every organization pays for backup personnel, whether you have them or not. Often, the organizations without backup personnel suffer serious consequences when a key person leaves the organization, is reassigned, or gets sick. Accept the fact that people do and will always leave the organization, for various reasons, be reassigned, quit, or have to take leaves because of illness. It is not a question of whether you need backup personnel but of when you will need them.

Once again, this is a strategic decision on the part of the program manager, but sometimes the hands of the program manager are tied. In the likely event that backup personnel cannot be assigned, the program manager must insist and make sure that adequate documentation exists for all projects. Additionally, establishing a formal "peer review" process, whereby every project manager has an assigned peer within the program and periodically (weekly or monthly or at major milestones) the peer must be individually briefed on the status of the project, can minimize the impact when a project manager is lost. Now someone else in the organization is at least familiar with the intimacies of the project.

How Strategies Are Designed to Ensure Organizational Discipline

The program manager needs to have a strategy for instilling discipline throughout the organization. Two overriding factors are involved in any kind of organizational discipline: (1) compliance of everyone in the organization because of the desire to please the leadership, and (2) compliance because of the fear of pain (negative repercussions).

Creating the kind of culture in which the organization has a desire to please the leadership hinges on relationship building. The strategies that provide pain when there is a lack of discipline in the organization are also required. Both approaches are required to maximize success, because all people are not alike. In any organization you'll have a percentage of people who will test the boundaries, and crossing some of these boundaries should lead to negative consequences for those who do so. Pain is often the most effective motivator for instilling discipline. For example, if someone willfully or callously violates a safety rule, punishment is in order. An organization left to its own actions in the absence of leadership (personal or process) will not have any discipline and will be doomed to failure.

Many paths lead to program success. The key is having the discipline to stick to the path. While the mentoring process and the status process contribute to discipline, the program manager acting with integrity contributes to discipline even more so. Realize that discipline is best when it is self-regulating. Therefore, having a certain amount of pride in yourself and in the organization is a powerful way to instill discipline in others. Instilling pride within an organization is absolutely necessary.

Organizational pride can and should be built. Frequently, organizations that have a lot of pride built into them appear as "arrogant" to outsiders. This is a criticism that has been labeled on

NASA (justly or unjustly), using a variety of terms in several outside audits. I have also heard people refer to the Walt Disney World company as arrogant. Many athletes at the top of their field are also called arrogant. The point is, if you do things with confidence and pride, someone will definitely call you arrogant. While arrogance is often considered a negative trait, in this case it is simply reflective of positive pride and is a trait that characterizes those who aspire to and accomplish great things.

Symbolism is something else you can use to instill discipline. A program manager I worked with kept a sign in his office that read: "No job is complete until the paperwork is done." Stories work well to instill discipline. It is commonly accepted that stories help maintain the culture of a society and they can also maintain or create the culture of an organization. Every organization usually has its share of good and bad stories. The good news is you only have to tell people and remind them of a few select good stories.

How to Mix Project Management Responsibilities with Organizational Responsibilities

Some programs have full-time project managers. Others mix project management and operational responsibilities. When you have a mix of operational and project management responsibilities, you have someone serving two masters.

Both sides (operations and project management) often underestimate the role and challenge of the other. Operations experience is very valuable and can make project managers well-rounded. However, operations responsibilities can be extremely time-consuming, especially when there are problems and issues. The decision of whether to mix operations and project management can hinge on the function and role of operations, but be sure not to overburden your project managers. Additionally, when people have dual responsibilities, like operations and project management, they often gravitate to the one they are most comfortable with, sometimes at the expense of the other.

When personnel have such split responsibilities, between project management and operations, the program should establish goals that serve as guidelines for what percentage of time the person should spend on operations and what percentage of time on project management. The goal doesn't have to be rigid, and a range works well. The program manager also needs to periodically follow up to ensure that adequate time is being spent on each objective and that the goals are appropriate for the situation. When dual responsibilities come into play, program managers must give more leadership than usual. The program manager needs to be readily available when guidance is required to strike the proper balance between these conflicting responsibilities.

How to Determine the Percentage of Organizational Resources to Spend on Operations/Maintenance versus Development

Every program with ongoing operations and maintenance has a ratio of its operations and maintenance costs to its development cost for new projects. You need to carefully measure and track this ratio over time. This ratio tells a story over time. Regardless of what the ratio actually is, the program manager must think strategically about what it should be, as programs can err on either side.

A lot of organizations maintain things that do not need to be maintained, or do not need to be maintained at that level. This can be especially true in the information technology environment, since some information technology personnel enjoy maintenance—especially on their "pet" applications—more than working on new projects. But nothing comes for free. Maintenance has a price, just as lack of maintenance has a price. Therefore, I recommend that you examine different ratios and determine the ramifications and

TABLE 4.1 Percentage of Program Resources

NEW DEVELOPMENT	MAINTENANCE	RAMIFICATIONS
20	80	?
40	60	?
50	50	?
60	40	?
80	20	?

impacts of each, including where the program is today and where it needs to go. Table 4.1 illustrates how to track the ramifications of varying program resource allotments.

The key is that this ratio should not be haphazardly obtained, but should be determined by a strategic decision on the part of the organization. A good guideline is to review this percentage mix twice a year to assess how well the organization is performing against the established goal. This should be part of the normal resource management process established by the program manager. Additionally, it is always good to periodically scrub items every year or two to see what can be reduced or eliminated. A "scrub" is essentially a bottom-up" detailed review of a process to ensure that the process is still valid and to identify improvement opportunities. The scrub itself can be managed as a project and is a good opportunity for a junior project manager to get more experience, as the scrub educates them on operations and maintenance, making them more well rounded.

How Project Management Administrative Functions Are Assigned

Project administration functions are different than project management functions. By administration functions I mean inputting the project parameters into the project management software, scheduling meetings, issuing minutes, compiling and expediting all the documentation and deliverables for the project, and providing the obligatory "courteous" follow-up on late tasks and deliverables. When project managers have to manage projects and do administrative functions, it is a very tough task, because the amount of work involved in administrative functions can be overwhelming. The non-administrative project management functions are much more important. Thus project managers who have to do both tend to fall behind, or they ignore or do not perform administrative functions, especially since the consequences of doing so are delayed.

The project management software in use today is very sophisticated with a lot of capability. Project management software packages usually add new features, capabilities, or other changes every year or two, which makes the products even more challenging to use. Most project managers understand and can use less than a tenth of this capability—they learn (often painfully) just enough to get their project tasks into the system. And a two- or three-day class or online tutorial doesn't make you proficient in the use of these tools. Granted, the training will provide the basis for building proficiency, but that is true only if you use the tool frequently after the training is completed. The tool is a small part of good project management, and unfortunately, most organizations have their project managers operating on the wrong end of the learning curve. As such, their project managers never get proficient or effective at using the tool, and in fact the project managers view the tool as a burden versus something that makes their job easier.

Realize that knowing the tool and performing all the necessary project management tasks is information/capability overload for the typical project manager. In fact, the skill set and natural ability to become proficient in the use of the project management software is different than the skill set and natural ability needed to be a great project manager, which is primarily people- and relationship-driven. It is a rare individual who is highly effective at both, because of personal preferences and time limitations. Time spent at the desktop with the tool is not time spent dealing with the myriad of project stakeholders.

The program manager needs to make the strategic decision of whether to split the two functions. When the functions are split, you have dedicated project administrators who work for and serve project managers. This means you can heavily invest in "tool" training for the administrators and make them experts on your project management software and methodology. Relieving your project managers of the administrative burdens allows them to work on more projects. Additionally, project administrators can serve more than one project manager. The project administrator also frees the project manager from a lot of the time spent generating and updating status. For example, very often, seven project managers and three project administrators accomplish more and provide better customer service than ten project managers all doing the project management and the administrative functions.

Project administrators need to be capable and have a customer focus (the project managers are their customers). If you choose not to have separate functions for project administration and project management, then consider making a subset of the project managers expert in the project management software tools so they can serve as mentors to the other project managers. The only challenge of maintaining tool expertise is that the software is frequently upgraded and/or changed every couple of years, and sometimes the organization changes tools.

How to Grow Organizational Capabilities by Increasing the Capabilities of Project Managers

In addition to meeting program goals, the program manager is challenged to grow the organization's capabilities by increasing the capabilities of program personnel, especially the project managers. This means planning for and making time for training and development opportunities. Setting developmental goals for personnel is also important. To that end, the program manager has to establish a culture that allows people to make and learn from their mistakes. Structures and processes for mentoring need to be established, and processes that provide feedback on performance and behavior should be put in place.

This feedback should come from the customers, peers, and program manager. Rotational assignments are also very important in broadening the perspective and experience base of program managers. But not all rotational assignments are created equally.

SCENARIO

NASA has had great success in developing leaders through its "Bubba" program. The more politically correct name of the program is the Executive Intern Program, but it started as "Bubba" before it became politically incorrect. The original name was "Bubba" because Bubba (the executive intern) would do whatever the executive required. The leader who spearheaded and popularized this Bubba program throughout NASA essentially created/developed a lot of NASA's current leadership, including two NASA Center directors and an astronaut.

The advantage of the Bubba program lies in its structure. The Bubba goes everywhere the leader goes and hears everything the leader hears, with the very rare exception of extremely sensitive issues. This requires trustworthiness on the part of the Bubba, but that is also a key element of leadership. The Bubba even travels with the executive, and as a result he or she meets all of the organization's executive-level leadership in formal and informal settings. Once the stint as Bubba is up (usually after six to eighteen months), the person goes back to his or her original position, but more frequently one of the other leaders the person has encountered offers the former Bubba a greater opportunity. More important, the Bubba has gone from an individual with a knot-hole view of the organization to someone that has an organization-wide perspective. The Bubba has had the opportunity to demonstrate his or her capabilities and strengths to the highest-level leadership in the organization.

Another opportunity for developing organizational capability is to make project managers owners of program processes. Have these processes assessed and scrubbed, and then rotate the owner-ship of the process. This results in project managers taking a "program perspective."

How to Balance Process and People

One of the biggest strategic decisions a program manager has to make is how much process to deploy. It is important to distinguish between rules and guidelines when establishing project management processes. For instance, it can be a rule that sign-off occurs at a stage gate, but the content of what is signed off at the gate is based on guidelines. It is difficult for any organization to establish rules that apply to everything without becoming bureaucratically intractable. Guidelines allow the use of "judgment" by project managers and actually foster accountability.

I have a client who has a rule that all projects of less than 1 million euros must produce a requirements document, but what that document is, the level of detail and structure it requires, is left up to the project manager, who is accountable for its sufficiency. The project manager partners this level of detail and structure with the program manager and stakeholders.

Ideally, there should be very few rules compared with the number of guidelines. Most rule-intensive processes I have encountered are not actually used to accomplish the work and are just brought out and dusted off for audits, used to try to impress unsuspecting customers, or become the favorite excuse for not achieving goals and objectives. The program manager has to strike a balance between process and people.

People dependence means the organization depends on the ability of its people to properly execute work activities and tasks. *Process dependence* means the organization depends on processes to ensure the proper execution of work activities and tasks. Figure 4.1 illustrates the necessity for balance of these two ideas.

FIGURE 4.1 Balance of People Dependence and Process Dependence

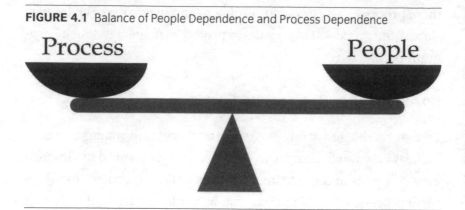

Often, organizations start out with very little process and are highly people-dependent. Eventually, because people are human, someone makes a mistake and there is a cry to create a process to prevent a recurrence of the mistake. Unfortunately, a lot of organizations overreact and create too many and/or too restrictive processes that actually prevent work from being accomplished. Organizations with good, active leadership often swing back and forth over time until a comfortable balance is struck, as illustrated in Figure 4.2.

Look at the advantages and disadvantages of being heavily people-dependent. Table 4.2 gives a breakdown of the advantages and disadvantages of a people-dependent culture.

Now look at the advantages and disadvantages of being heavily process-dependent, as illustrated in Table 4.3.

A lot of factors go into how process- or people-dependent an organization or work segment needs to be. These factors include the criticality of the operation, as well as the availability and ability of the people performing the work. The true test of the validity and effectiveness of the program's processes is whether people actually use the processes to do the work. Or conversely, do they have to work around the process to accomplish the task?

FIGURE 4.2. Achieving a Comfortable Process-People Balance

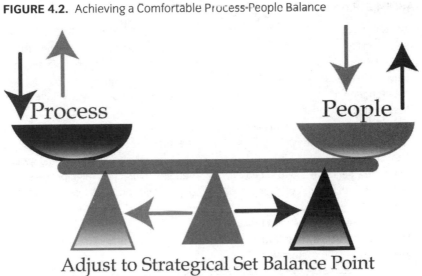

TABLE 4.2 People Dependency

ADVANTAGES	DISADVANTAGES
• Gives workers satisfaction	• Higher risks
• Nimble	• Can provide a "false sense" of a high
• Flexible	degree of control
• Adaptable	• Less repeatability
• Efficient	• Makes customers nervous
• Helps retain high-achieving confident	• Turnover impacts much greater
people	
• Speed	
• Requires more and strict planning for	
backup of key personnel	

Establishing a Process-People Balance

Some books and maturity models advocate high degrees of process as the goal. The program manager has to weigh the advantages of more process against the organizational goals, objectives,

TABLE 4.3 Process Dependency

ADVANTAGES	DISADVANTAGES
• Repeatability • Easier to improve processes that allow benefits to be readily achieved across the organization • Less people dependence • More flexibility in assignments and developmental activities • Predictability • Brings new personnel up to speed faster and with less risk of poor performance • Better able to handle complex projects • Instills confidence in organizational leadership and the customer	• Paperwork can overshadow the task • Resources must be spent enforcing or ensuring compliance • Someone must own and manage the process • Causes people to check their brain at the door • Thinking analytically is work and gets better with practice; high-process dependency provides less "thinking" practice

risks, and resources available. A process maturity model may help with this, but in the program environment, there are so many dynamics and variables that to arbitrarily say we should be a level three or four or five on some maturity scale is risky. The following are keys to help establish a balanced process.

- The program manager must listen to the process. What does the current circumstance tell us about the process? Every problem that occurs is telling you something about the process. The program manager must think in terms of "Could a more rigorous process have prevented this problem?" The answer is not always to have more process. Even when the answer is more process, you need to assess the benefit/cost ratio for the additional process.

- Get feedback on the process. Ask the process users to critique the process for both positive and negative attributes. This should be a standard part of lessons-learned discussions that occur at major milestones.

- Don't create or maintain processes the organization does not use to accomplish the work. Many organizations have processes in their systems that people don't use to accomplish the work, or they only use a very small part of it. This is more common in organizations that have or create process to which there is no process owner.

- Processes tend to migrate or slowly change over time and require periodic scrubbing and evaluation. Processes should be formally reviewed every year to eighteen months. Significant processes should have a change control process that allows users to submit proposed process changes.

- There should always be a way to handle waivers or exceptions to the process when the process needs to be violated. The program manager should have full authority to adjust or change the process. This includes the authority to eliminate or shortcut processes as required. While this may seem like anarchy to organizations with a strong PMO, until the PMO is accountable for cost and schedule targets, full authority should lie with the program manager. The PMO and program managers must work together to establish usable process and make improvements or changes where compliance is problematic. Realize that no process or procedure is perfect, nor can it apply to every circumstance. Sometimes the process has to be violated. When a preplanned violation occurs, paperwork should be processed. The paperwork is typically called an "exception" or a "waiver." To initiate the exception or waiver, an e-mail to the approving authority, usually the program manager and/or process owner, is acceptable. Failure to do this minimizes opportunities to improve the process, because the number and type of exceptions and waivers would tell you about deficiencies in the process. Even more important, without formal documentation, program personnel will begin to casually violate the process to the degree the process becomes invalid.

- Processes may be unique or tailored within each program or even project at the discretion of the program manager. The program manager must decide to tailor a few to many processes or waiver a single or few processes.
- The more diversified or global the program elements, the more important process becomes, and the more important the adaptability of the processes becomes.

Traits of an Effective Process Strategy

Many models can gauge project management process maturity. There is nothing inherently wrong with these maturity models, but keep in mind that the models are generic. They cannot apply to all situations, and many organizations may be at varying levels of maturity depending upon the purview or aspect to which the model is applied or from which the organization is viewed. With that said, the following list reveals the tips that are applicable for any process maturity level.

- Leadership recognizes that the process is a strategy.
- People follow the process to accomplish the work.
- The process instills discipline, integrity, and accountability.
- There is a single owner for each process, and he or she is known to the organization.
- There is a change control method for the process.
- The process has an "appeal" method by which process violations are approved and documented for special circumstances.

- The process is periodically scrubbed, and the results are briefed to leadership.

The program manager is charged with making program process strategic decisions that impact on long-term program health while dealing with real-time tactical issues. Most actions that program managers take have both strategic and tactical ramifications. The program manager must remain cognizant of the strategic direction in which he or she is driving the program with regard to program processes.

KEYSTONES
Program Process Strategy

1. People and projects will come and go, but the program culture remains and needs to be managed.
2. As a leader, you must assess the culture you create for your project managers and implement changes that are not just quick fixes to single instances or problems, but that have positive long-term effects on the culture.
3. Program managers are required to pick the organization's pain and shortcomings. To do so, the program manager has to strike balances among opposing objectives.
4. A consistent and effective status process is the keystone of a stable program culture, which should help project managers be successful.
5. If people are not being assessed, graded, or rewarded for mentoring, you cannot expect mentoring to occur.
6. The program manager must think strategically about how project managers are assigned.
7. Every organization pays for backup personnel, whether you have them or not.
8. The program manager needs to have a strategy for instilling discipline throughout the organization.
9. Program managers must provide more leadership to project managers, who also have organizational responsibility.
10. The amount of time and resources spent on maintenance versus development is a strategic decision.

11. Consideration should be given to splitting the project management and project administration functions.
12. Organizational capabilities increase when the capability of project managers increases.
13. A strategic balance between people dependence and process dependence must be achieved and adjusted.
14. Processes should have rules and guidelines that provide flexibility based on the circumstances.
15. A key test for process assessment is to verify that people follow the processes to accomplish the work.

Program Execution Processes

Execution means actually going out and implementing what has been planned. Good execution requires a plan. Without a plan, you cannot judge the effectiveness of execution. This seems obvious, but a lot of programs are continually in a state of "fire fighting" because there is no real plan. These program managers subconsciously and inappropriately judge their effectiveness by how many fires are burning out of control. Even in dynamic environments you must have a plan or a series of short plans tailored to the rapidly changing environment. I am continually amused by the organizational leader who hears or reads about Earned Value and wants to implement it immediately, only to discover that it requires a valid plan to be meaningful. Their organization struggles with its implementation because their plans are not credible.

Establish an Appropriate Planning Horizon

The planning horizon is the timeframe for the amount of work you can reasonably schedule based on project requirements and availability of resources. If the project requirements are not stable, you cannot produce a stable schedule. Often only a certain percentage or portion of the requirements is stable. In this case, the program manager needs to assess the validity of the requirements over the timeframe of the project. It is perplexing to see detailed 18- to 24-month schedules for an IT development project. What are the odds that the details that exist in the schedule will actually be used 18 months or more from now? In most cases, it's very slim! So why burden the organization with defining and/or creating detail that in all probability will not be used? Effective project management means knowing what to ignore as well as what to pay attention to, and the program manager has to give project managers the guidance and the freedom to do this.

The other factor that reduces the planning horizon is instability of available resources required to execute the plan. Resources are required to complete tasks; therefore, the program manager needs to spend significant time resolving resource conflicts and issues in order to establish a stability window for project managers. Realize that you cannot effectively plan beyond the project's planning horizon. For some organizations, the planning horizon may be a week, for others it may be a month, and for some others still it may be a year.

When establishing a planning horizon, first examine all the current project schedules within the program. Assess the validity of these schedules week by week. "Validity" means that the work is planned and the resources are assigned. How many weeks into the future you have a valid schedule for is your planning horizon. This then dictates how frequently you must replan. So if your planning horizon is a week, then replanning must occur weekly as well.

If your planning horizon is a month, then replanning must also occur monthly. The planning horizon is your "stability" window.

Next, assess what prevents you from extending the planning horizon. Is it a resource issue? Or is it a requirements or stakeholder issue? In general, a longer planning horizon results in a more stable work environment, which in turn increases the satisfaction and effectiveness of all participants. To accomplish this, the program manager must assess all the items that prevent extending the planning horizon, decide which obstacles should be fixed, and then put in strategies and tactics to fix what should be fixed. I use the expression "should be fixed" here because you may decide that the obstacle preventing extension of the planning horizon shouldn't be fixed, and therefore your maximum planning horizon is two weeks (or whatever timeframe is relevant for your company) based on the constraints you have. Whatever your timeframe is, you need to know it, because it is something you need to constantly communicate to your team. When people understand *why* the planning horizon is two weeks, they'll feel less frustration and will be able to better plan their own work activities.

The length of your planning horizon can be dependent on the maturity of your organization or the type of business environment you are in. The program manager needs to constantly look for ways to extend the planning horizon. Organizations that attempt to plan beyond the planning horizon typically have disappointed and discontented program personnel, because these people end up spending a significant portion of time planning things that never happen.

Spiral development cycles and *agile project management* both attempt to address very short planning horizons. Agile project management attempts to create iterative and incremental deliveries while supposedly being adaptive as opposed to anticipatory. Spiral development essentially integrates design and prototyping in stages with incremental deliveries. There is no magic in either of these philosophies.

Many organizations falsely assume that to use something like Agile or Spiral means that everything else is tossed out the window. Program managers have to be astute enough to examine and extract what is beneficial from any methodology or management mantra. It is usually the consultant or salesperson who wants you to "buy" the whole thing. Project management is still structured, organized common sense whether you are using Agile or Spiral philosophies or some other rationales to plan each iteration of a project with goals and deliverables. In actuality, these processes, which some people view or "sell" as easier, are more work because they increase the number of planning cycles.

Simply stated, it is just common sense not to plan in detail or execute beyond your planning horizon. You do not need a consultant, a "new" methodology, or a special software package to do it. I am a proponent of thoroughly examining your circumstances and constraints and then aggressively deploying common sense. Your circumstances and constraints involve the elements of cost, scope, and schedule. The scheduling methods described next address different ways of executing by making trade-offs among these constraints.

Establish a Scheduling Philosophy

The planning horizon is a reality that poses a challenge in the creation of schedules and delivery dates. Traditionally, organizations often use the *critical path method* to establish project schedules, even though this method assumes unlimited resources. The "critical path" shows the longest path of project tasks that result in the shortest possible schedule. But the critical path method will not produce a valid schedule in a resource-constrained environment because it is not resource-leveled and the critical path method assumes unlimited resources. In a matrix, or shared-resource environment, a lot of program managers try to focus on critical path when the focus really needs to be on resource allocation. On a resource-leveled schedule for a project, it is possible to have a different critical path every week or even more frequently. Resource leveling means to create a valid schedule based on the resources you have available.

There are two main types of resource leveling: (1) time-constrained resource leveling, and (2) resource-constrained resource leveling. As a program manager, you need to determine which type to use for new projects.

In time-constrained resource leveling, the end date is fixed and resources are added to the project until the desired end date or critical path method end date is achievable. With time-constrained resource leveling, time is more important than money. Examples of time-constrained resource leveling were all the Y2K, or year 2000, information technology projects that had to be completed by the turn of the century. The end date was fixed and organizations threw resources at the problem to make sure they made the end date.

Resource-constrained resource leveling maintains a cap or limit on the amount of resources, and the project end date slips so the resources can remain below the cap. So the schedule delivery date is based on the resources allocated for the project. If the cap or limit on the allocation is raised, a shorter schedule may be obtained.

Fixed Delivery-Date Scheduling

A popular variation of time-constrained resource leveling is fixed delivery-date scheduling. In fixed delivery-date scheduling the resources may or may not be capped, but the end date is fixed. To accommodate the end date, the requirements may be adjusted. So the project begins with the project manager and stakeholders putting all the requirements in priority order. As the project progresses toward the end date, the project manager constantly assesses the team's ability to deliver all the requirements and eliminate as many requirements as necessary to hold the delivery date. Obviously they eliminate the requirements judged to be lower priority. After delivery, the list of eliminated requirements is integrated with any new requirements, and the process starts all over again. The advantage of this method is that it stabilizes the operational environment. Training and implementation can be better planned.

For example, a program manager in an information technology organization told me that his organization had always planned four releases per year, but because of schedule delays the release date would often slip. When the release date slipped, there would always be one or more stakeholders with a "hot" requirement that now had to be squeezed into the release. This further complicated things, and the release would also have to be recoordinated around operational constraints. So although they planned for four releases per year, they typically delivered three, and in one tough year they barely squeezed out two. Since they went to fixed delivery-date scheduling, they have not missed a scheduled release in over two and a half years and have regained customer confidence. Even though the customers don't always get all the requirements they wanted in that release, they have confidence in the next release date.

Rolling-Wave Scheduling

Still another way to accommodate a planning horizon that is shorter than project duration is to use "rolling wave" scheduling, which essentially establishes a planning horizon whereby a detailed project schedule is generated for the planning horizon (the current wave) and a general direction with major tasks is maintained for the remainder of the project (future waves). During the execution of this scheduling period, planning for the next scheduling period takes place. This continues until the project is complete. There is also the traditionally accepted method of scheduling projects in which the entire project schedule is planned at the beginning.

All program managers need to give adequate consideration to the chosen execution paths for projects. And realize that all projects within a program don't have to follow the same execution strategy. For example, a program's top-priority projects may be time constrained, with program resources allocated to these projects to meet these dates. Projects of lesser priority may have their end dates slide to accommodate the fact that there aren't sufficient resources to accommodate all the project tasks. The program manager's responsibility for execution begins by establishing the scheduling plans for projects in the program. This is a conscious decision that has to be made based on the priority of the projects, the resources available, the planning horizon, and the organizational constraints. This is a key aspect of setting up a culture that fosters project success.

Implement a Stage Gate Process to Ensure Proper Execution of the Planned Schedule

Scheduling provides a plan of work flow, which is managed by the organization's project management processes. Whether the organization has lots of processes and is heavily process-dependent or it has few processes and is mostly people-dependent, it is necessary to ensure adherence to whatever processes there are. This is best done using stage gates.

A "stage gate" is essentially a checkpoint in the project management process. The project is not allowed to proceed past the checkpoint without demonstrating the necessary "proof" of readiness to proceed. So at each stage gate the program manager and/or the PMO define what deliverables the project must have before it can go on. This ensures both compliance and thoroughness. Additionally, a major side benefit of the stage gate process is that when something is missing or inadequate, the project cannot proceed. Now you have an automatic escalation method for program manager intervention because the project is essentially "on hold" or in a state of "work stoppage" until the issue is resolved.

Project managers get into trouble when they yield to pressure to proceed even though there are unresolved issues or work items that should have been put to bed early in the project management process. Once project managers understand the stage gate process, they realize it is both a friend and a weapon. In other words, when a customer or other powerful stakeholders pressure the project manager to cut corners or proceed while having unresolved issues, the stage gate process allows the manager to say, "The stage gate process does not allow us to proceed at this point without having this deliverable. We can go to the program manager, who can process a waiver or exception, but I can't proceed on my own."

When these issues come to the program manager, it is an integrity moment. Judgment is always paramount, and an exception may be warranted. However, in most cases it is up to the program manager to hold the organization's feet to the fire and instill the discipline the process requires. Expect that when the stage gate process is first implemented, there will be a lot of push-back until the organization realizes that the process is for real and for their benefit. Just like children who are not used to discipline and find it uncomfortable at first, so will the organization. Expect to hear some whining and maybe even a temper tantrum or two. That's why the program manager and project managers need to treat the stage gate process with formality and intestinal fortitude (guts). You must adhere to it as a process and formally approve any exceptions. Without this kind of rigor the stage gate process will degrade over time into something that just exists on paper, and the stakeholders won't respect it.

Balance between Control and Bureaucracy

After everyone is committed to the stage gate process, you need to determine the number of gates the process will use. Once again, you need to strike a balance between control and bureaucracy. Depending on your organization or program, you could have 50 gates or 5 gates. There could be a set number of gates for all projects, or there may be tiered levels of control depending upon project size and complexity. These are program management decisions.

Major milestones are the natural places to establish stage gates. Some organizations even establish the gate in front of the milestone by a few weeks, or they have a milestone readiness review. Since milestones can be big events for customers and stakeholders, be sure to resolve any issues before the formal milestone. Stage gates help out with this.

Regarding milestones, progress before the milestone seems to adhere to the 80/20 rule. That is, often it seems that 80 percent of the work is accomplished in the 20 percent of the time right before the milestone. Why does that happen? It is because milestones create pressure to accomplish work. Every project has a natural set of milestones. The program manager should examine the project's milestones to see if there are opportunities to insert additional milestones if there are large or significant gaps between natural milestones. The inserted milestones can be "program audit," "external review," or "design 75 percent complete." The added milestone forces an assessment, and the assessment forces work to get done.

Evaluate the Process

A review of stage gate deliverables can be completed by the program manager, or it can be a series of self-checks whereby the project manager signs off or certifies that all the deliverables a stage gate requires are complete, or it can be peer reviewed, in which case project managers sign off on each other's readiness to proceed to the next gate. Signature accountability is important here. Occasionally auditing any self-checks is also warranted.

Maintain Integrity with Change Control

Lack of full consideration of the impact a change has on a project and/or program often results in major problems. When changes are evaluated for consideration in modifying the baselined requirements, all impacts need to be assessed against all elements of the triple constraint and all stakeholders.

Track the change history over time for projects within the program, as it provides a measure of the requirements' stability and is in fact a metric of how well project teams did prior to baselining the requirements. The 80/20 rule, or Pareto Analysis should be conducted for the program's proposed requirements changes. In this case, the 80/20 rule essentially says that 20 percent of the requirements often account for 80 percent of the changes. When you see these kinds of trends, you want to aggressively find out why these changes are being made. It could be symptomatic of a larger problem with this portion of the requirements or a generic problem that has yet to surface in other areas of the requirements. The first set of changes that occur after the requirements have been baselined and need to be examined for cause and effect.

Some common project change drivers include:

- Changes in business needs/requirements driven by project management or project stakeholders
- Changes in the business environment (competitive actions, new technologies, and new processes)
- Changes due to problems or opportunities that occur during the course of the project

- Changes due to modifications or enhancements identified by the project team (within project scope)
- Changes due to faults detected by the project team or users

Your change management process should be designed so that it's intentionally cumbersome. I know that may not sound customer-friendly, but it is actually for the customer's own protection.

For example, most dentists advertise "pain free" dentistry. However, going to the dentist is not at the top on my priority list. In fact, when I have a tooth that exhibits some pain, I don't immediately schedule an appointment with my dentist. I will test the tooth with hot and cold foods for a few days. If the tooth continues to give me pain or if the pain gets more serious, then I schedule an appointment with my "pain free" dentist. When my dentist gives me the pain-free shot, he says that I might feel a little stick and then a little pressure.

The change control process should be "pain free," just like the dentist is supposed to be. Your customer should feel a little stick and a little pressure. In other words, just as I give full consideration to whether or not my tooth pain truly requires the dentist, you want the customer to give full consideration to whether he or she really needs that change. Is it worth going through the change control process? Fortunately, it is difficult to implement an adequate change control process that isn't cumbersome. So make sure your process is both customer-friendly and cumbersome.

The program manager must ensure that her or his project managers practice adequate change control. This is effectively established through a change control board (CCB). A CCB is necessary even for small projects. The board can consist of just the project manager, or it could be chaired by the program manager and include project managers and major stakeholders. The structure of the CCB needs to match the criticality and significance of the project to the program, and it should be approved by the program manager. Realize that it is impossible to do adequate change control unless there is a baseline that serves as a reference point.

Emphasize the Baseline

Baselining the requirements is a big deal and should be treated as such. This baseline serves as the control point for the requirements, anchoring the project and the team. The baseline is the focal point for all project decisions. The scope or requirements baseline can be maintained separately, but the project baseline includes all aspects of the triple constraint in addition to scope. The baselining of the requirements is typically a stage gate and provides the program manager an opportunity to notify all stakeholders that from this point forward they will be adhering to a strict change control process. This provides some relief from pressure for the project managers and emphasizes the seriousness of the change control process to project stakeholders. The baselining process should prepare customers for change control.

The program manager should train project managers to never say or use the word "requirements" with stakeholders and customers. With a strong baselining process, there are only "preliminary" requirements and "baselined" requirements. Consistent use of the qualifiers "preliminary" and "baselined" psychologically prepares the customer and other stakeholders for the baselining process. It reinforces the fact that all requirements are preliminary until baselined and that any requirement that "pops up" after the baseline is not in scope by definition and is treated as preliminary until it goes through the change control process. Some programs never get a good handle on their requirements because the customer doesn't take the initial requirements process seriously and continually submits new requirements after the baseline with full expectation of pain-free inclusion.

It is up to the program manager to establish and approve the chairing process for the change control boards. There can be tiered approval levels for this process. This means the project manager may be authorized to approve changes within prede- fined boundaries. The escalation process should be clear when scope, cost, or schedule impacts exceed approved tolerance levels. It is important that no changes be allowed outside of the change control process.

Realize that there will be circumstances that may require "real- time" or near-real-time approval for project changes. That's why the program manager should make sure the process identifies who has authority for "out-of-board" approvals and what are the limits of that authority. The chairman can also coordinate change approvals with CCB members if the magnitude of the change is not significant enough to warrant face-to-face meetings. There should also be someone designated to act as the alternate CCB chairman to handle out-of-board changes in the event the primary chairman is unavailable. The number of out-of-board approvals of change requests should be minimal if the change control board is meeting frequently enough. Not meeting frequently enough can cause work to be delayed and people to work outside or around the change control system. On very large-scale projects or pro- grams it is not uncommon to meet daily. Use your best judgment.

Use a Change Control Form

There is always a lot of discussion and debate in my classes about the necessity of the change request form. The common question is "What if I have an e-mail from the customer? Do I still need a form?" Yes! Every change should be on a change request form. Use of the form communicates to the entire community the serious- ness of the change control process. Earlier I mentioned that the change control process must be cumbersome and customer-friendly. If the customer sends a change request in an e-mail, the project manager should prepare the change request form for the customer to sign to make the process customer-friendly. The form maintains process integrity. Once you start allowing e-mails and notes, traceability and accountability become problematic. You have to treat the process with respect in order for others to treat it with respect.

Create a Status Process That Allows You to Regulate Execution

A project status process is one of the greatest opportunities to establish a positive, disciplined project management culture. In fact, if you exist in an environment that has poor or nonexistent project management processes, the first process that should be rolled out and matured is the project status process.

The status monitoring process yields benefits beyond delivering projects successfully organization-wide. Without the integrity that results from a "project status awareness culture," success exists only in pockets of the organization that have excellent project managers. As a consultant who has observed the "innards" of many companies, large and small, renowned and unknown, I can attest that an organization's method of monitoring project status is a key indicator of that organization's project management quality. I am sure Ronald Reagan had the project status process in mind when he said, "Trust but verify." These three words sum up the purpose of a good project status process.

Some organizations view project status as a necessary evil, which is needed just to satisfy incessant requests from management. Proactive leaders, however, view project status as a critical process that adds value to project management and facilitates communication with senior management, project partners, and customers. Project status monitoring should be viewed as a process at the core of discipline and integrity throughout the entire project management organization.

Project Status Best Practices

Five characteristics of effective project management are common to most evaluation techniques.

1. *Consistency*—The status process should be basically the same for large and small projects, and consistent with their measures of success.
2. *Escalation*—The status process should provide a mechanism for escalation of key issues.
3. *Simple*—The status process sheet should be on one page but with the ability to drill down for details when necessary.
4. *Public*—The status process should be available to all (as appropriate) in order to communicate issues, risks, and corrective action measures.
5. *Inclusive*—The status process should be a requirement of all projects.

Ten Obstacles to Effective Project Status

1. How status should be reported is always changing and there are frequent requests for "special" reports and/or briefings that are outside of the normal, accepted standards and processes.
2. Status reviews are not held on a regular, consistent basis— same time, same place, same leadership.
3. There is inconsistent status reporting to management from project to project, causing difficulty in interpreting status.

4. Leaders are too busy to review or accept status.
5. Status is reported at the detail level instead of in a summary.
6. Project managers are too busy working the project and fighting fires to monitor status.
7. Projects are not structured or organized for status metrics to be easily available.
8. At the start of the project, there is no education of stakeholders to achieve "buy-in" on how status will be monitored.
9. There is overreliance on status metrics by management, without a "feel" for what is actually taking place in the project.
10. Too much time is wasted on the status of stable projects and not enough time is spent on projects that are at risk.

Some companies have project failures because the leadership is made aware of a troublesome project too late to resolve the issue or to improve the situation without dire consequences. Such problems can be identified early as part of the project status process.

The Role of the Program Manager during Project Status Meetings

The program manager's attitudes and behavior set the tone for all stakeholders in the project status process. Therefore, consider the following:

1. Take the status process seriously. The project managers and the project teams reflect the program manager's respect for the process. Taking the status process meetings seriously means adhering rigorously to the meeting's scheduled date and time, and following a published agenda.

2. Focus on progress. Some organizations go so far as to call status meetings "progress meetings." The focus should be on the identification and resolution of challenges to progress so the project can proceed at the scheduled pace. Status meetings must be "forward-looking" and not allowed to degenerate into "finger-pointing" or "blaming" sessions.

3. Ferret out key issues. The leader must learn to ask effective questions. There is power in the public questioning of project managers and teams, because the questions that are raised publicly, in front of all of the project managers, eventually become the questions they raise internally before the leader asks those questions again.

4. Establish a positive culture. Provide praise and opportunity where appropriate. Allow lower-level personnel to present within their area of responsibility for their professional development and the development of future leaders.

5. Make timely decisions. Issues requiring a decision should get a decision at the project status meeting or, if it is beyond the program manager's control, a commitment to escalate the issue to the proper level for quick resolution. Actions and issues should be formally tracked to ensure timely decision making and thorough follow-up.

Project Status Meeting Frequency

The frequency of project status meetings can be weekly, biweekly, or monthly, depending on the project's duration and risk level. Daily status meetings may be held by the project manager for critical and/or troubled projects. A typical program calendar (Figure 5.1) and project status meeting agenda for a program or organizational unit (Table 5.1) are shown below.

FIGURE 5.1. Typical Program Calender

Typical Program Calendar						
Sunday	Monday	Tuesday	Wednesday	Thursday	Friday	Saturday
		Monthly Integrated Risk Review	Stage Gate Approval		Weekly Status	
			Program Level CCB		Weekly Status	
			Stage Gate Approval		Weekly Status	
			Program Level CCB		Weekly Status	

* Weekly Status Meetings include 1 to 5 detailed project reviews
* Consistent times need to be set aside daily for problem resolutions and exceptions

TABLE 5.1 Project Status Meeting Agenda

AGENDA ITEM	AVERAGE TIME
Meeting overview, attendance, validation of agenda items, special program/organizational announcements as required	Brief

OVERALL PROJECT STATUS

Project 1 status	≤3 minutes
Project 2 status	≤3 minutes
Project 3 status	≤3 minutes
Project . . . status	≤3 minutes
Project . . . status	≤3 minutes
Project . . . status	≤3 minutes
Project *n* status	≤3 minutes

DETAILED PROJECT REVIEWS

Project Alpha	20 to 60 minutes
Project Gamma	20 to 60 minutes

The presentation charts for overall project status should exactly represent the detailed status sheet. Use backup charts only as required. Not only does this avoid duplication of effort; it also emphasizes the importance of keeping information current and accurate. Therefore, the tool used to accomplish the task should be the same tool used in presentations. A lot of organizations waste significant time "preparing charts" for presentations, but when you use the tool it exposes leadership to the tool and sometimes helps identify process improvement opportunities.

Projects in good standing, with all aspects of the triple constraints in control, can be reviewed rapidly (typically in less than one minute). When this process is initially rolled out, the meeting will take longer, but when the project status process is mature, the project is healthy, and the leader is familiar with the project, the status summary report allows the leader to eyeball the chart in less than one minute and say, "Next project please."

A good project status meeting is really an "exception-focused activity" with discussion on what is off plan or off process. Therefore, if a project is in good standing and has no issues, a discussion is not warranted. These are the project status reviews that take less than a minute. The goal is to establish a project status culture in which leadership is not talking about what they could and should read for themselves, but rather they are addressing issues that require decisions, dissemination, or escalation.

Every project manager within the program should be ready for a detailed project presentation with a few days' notice or less. Projects should rotate through detailed presentations at the regularly scheduled project status meeting, at the discretion of the program manager or organizational leader. It is important to have detailed project presentations from projects that are in good standing, in addition to the projects that have challenges. A project in good standing may be reviewed in detail at quarterly meetings or at designated general status meetings.

TIP

Why perform detailed reviews of healthy projects? For one thing, it is risky for the program manager or organizational leader to assume that projects with good current status don't have hidden issues. Risk assessment should be an ongoing process. Additionally, detailed reviews of good projects provide opportunities for praise and demonstrate the characteristics of a project in good standing. This positive model counterbalances the usual focus on the negative.

The status meetings serve as the forum for critical decisions with regard to troubled projects. Sometimes decisions have to be escalated outside of this forum, but the general rule should be that decisions are made at the meeting. It is important to establish a culture that doesn't allow issues requiring decisions to persist without resolution, and a culture in which project managers know when and where to go for decisions beyond their control. Unfortunately, a number of organizations suffer because decisions either are not made, or are made in haphazard circumstances that are not migrated through the entire organization. The project status meeting is a decision tool and a communication tool that prevents those problems.

The Project Status Sheet

Figure 5.2 shows a typical project status sheet. (I have observed dozens of derivatives or variations of this format, proving that it can be tailored to the needs of any organization.)

Follow these guidelines for an effective project status sheet:

1. The project status sheet should be on one page. As with a resume or an e-mail, people rarely turn the page or scroll down to read lots of text. More important, it allows the readers to focus on what is important to them. You can pack a lot of information onto one page. Examine a Value

FIGURE 5.2 Typical Project Status Sheet

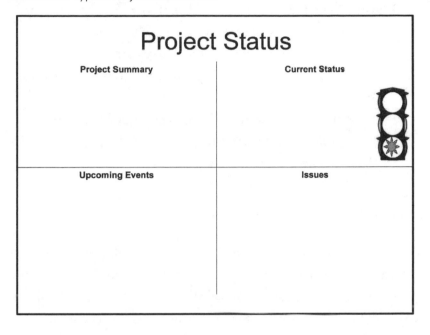

Line investment survey for your company or a company
that supports your organization. You can read that one
page for an hour. Busy executives and leaders don't have
the time and are typically not inclined to wade through
multipage status reports. If necessary, print the sheet using
a small type size to fit everything on a single page.

2. New information or information that is less than one
   month old should be typed in bold type to allow quick
   identification of what has changed since the previous
   reporting period. This saves significant time for the reader
   who knows the project.

3. The report is stand-alone and should provide a complete
   story without someone having to explain it. A good project status report provides a summary (including purpose)

of the project, current status, upcoming milestones, and issues. The four quadrants of the status report represent the old axiom, "Where we've been, where we are, where we are going, and what our challenges are."

4. Use symbols (like the stoplight symbol) to indicate overall status.

5. It should clearly identify who is accountable (the preparer), the date it was put together, and the preparer's telephone number and e-mail address.

Quadrant 1—Project Summary

The project summary quadrant states the overall purpose of the project and clearly relates it to the organization and/or company goals. This section answers all of the who, what, when, where, why, and how questions. A lot of this information comes directly from the business case. It also provides a reference or link to more information about the project, such as a project charter or project repository. Once this quadrant is complete, it rarely changes unless the business needs driving the project change, usually causing a rebaselining of the project, which should also be documented here. Even though this quadrant remains mostly static, it is important to include it because the organization and project team members are often not static, and this quadrant tells the new reader at a glance what the project is about.

Quadrant 2—Current Status

The current status quadrant clearly communicates the standing of the project. The cost baseline showing plan versus actual costs can use graphic or tabular format. The organization's valid (accurate and timely) earned value measures can appear here. Some organizations will even show a metric indicating the customer's "perception" of the project thus far, because this may not always be consistent with the project manager's perspective. The most important item in this quadrant is the symbol for the status of the project (usually a green, yellow, or red indicator). Clear criteria must be established for what makes a project green, yellow, or red. In addition to the overall project status indicator, some organizations show separate status indicators for the triple constraint (cost, schedule, and scope).

Quadrant 3—Upcoming Events

The upcoming events quadrant shows the planned activities and events for the short term (usually one to three months) and the major milestones beyond the short-term planning horizon. This quadrant provides a snapshot preview of what is on the plate of the project team over the near term.

Quadrant 4—Challenges and Issues

The challenges and issues quadrant provides a mechanism whereby the project manager and project team can notify management of challenges and issues, and more important to identify their approach to overcoming these challenges and resolving these issues. It also provides the opportunity to highlight where decisions or "higher-level influence" is necessary. Unfortunately, many projects produce less than desirable results because management does not provide critical decisions to project managers in a timely manner.

Management should be keenly aware of the necessary decisions and should be held accountable for making hard decisions that are required. This quadrant serves as a basis for driving accountability to both the project manager and his or her leadership. Project managers should be taught to be explicit about what decisions are needed. Note that this means project managers should provide multiple solutions with a recommended course of action for the program leadership to pick from.

Project Execution Success

Project status is a process that can instill discipline and integrity throughout an organization and ensure project success. It serves as a communications tool and facilitates the propagation of lessons-learned among participants. When project status monitoring permeates the culture, it saves the organization time by driving accountability and minimizing bureaucracy for quick, effective issue resolution.

Execution processes are extremely important. Project managers look to you—the program manager—to resolve issues that arise when the plan becomes reality. If the answers were easy, they wouldn't ask you.

Having a plan without the loyalty of the people to implement it is useless. You gain some loyalty by ensuring that the plan is realistic, and you gain the rest through communication. Therefore, the planning horizon should be defined and communicated to all stakeholders because it influences all decision processes. The schedules will be dictated by resource availability and the assumptions and methods the program manager uses to allocate these resources need to be communicated. Additionally, the stage gate, change control, and status processes need to be communicated and sold to the stakeholders. Execution might be humming along, but the program manager has to assure that project managers and stakeholders understand the who, what, why, when, where, and how behind the execution processes so they don't fight them.

Program Execution Processes

1. The planning horizon is the timeframe for the amount of work you can reasonably schedule based on project requirements and resource availability.
2. Effective project management means knowing what to ignore.
3. Good execution involves thoroughly examining your circumstances and constraints and then aggressively deploying common sense.
4. The program manager's responsibility for execution begins by establishing the scheduling plans for projects in the program.
5. Program and project managers need to treat the stage gate process with formality and intestinal fortitude (guts).
6. Your change management process should be designed so it is intentionally cumbersome and customer-friendly.
7. An effective status process allows you to regulate execution.
8. The program manager's attitudes and behavior set the tone for all stakeholders in the project management process.

Team Building at the Program Level

Strong teams don't just happen. They are made. Program managers have responsibility for teams on multiple levels and have to make sure project managers are capable of building strong teams.

Identify Teams

Before you can build a strong team, you must first identify one. The worst mistakes and problems are the ones that begin with "We didn't think about . . ." That's why the program manager needs to think about all the possible teams, internal and external, connected to the program. People take pride in being part of a team, but if no one identifies or recognizes the team, people find it difficult to participate or to have pride in being involved.

It is obvious that within a program the individual projects involve teams. Likewise, the operations segments may also be made up of teams. But what about the project managers themselves? Are they treated as a team, having associated team-building activities for them as a group? Or do you have a group of project managers who hardly know each other and who view and treat each other as adversaries engaged in constant "unfriendly" competition?

Project managers supporting the program are a team and need to be treated as such. The very profound but underutilized statement that "two heads are better than one" applies here. Most of the issues that your project managers face are similar or interrelated.

In a matrix environment, when you have functional managers that support your program, the program manager can view these functional managers as a team. Although by design their functions are different, a lot of the issues they face are common. And when the program manager periodically meets with his or her team of functional managers, great results can transpire.

Unfortunately, a lot of organizations suffer from overcommunication and are saturated with e-mails, directives, memos, circulars, etc.—most of which never even get read. I once worked for a very high-level leader who would often get frustrated with the volume of e-mail he received. To his assistants' and secretaries' dismay, he would occasionally and intentionally delete his entire e-mail Inbox and make the statement "If it is truly important, someone will come and get me."

TIP

Rather than simply sending e-mails to your team of functional managers, have a team meeting to bring them up to speed on program status and goals. The meeting provides a mechanism for issue identification and solutions, and allows you to reaffirm and strengthen their commitment to the program.

In addition to functional managers, you can treat other stakeholder groups as a team with associated benefits. For example, when appropriate, you can treat your suppliers as a team. This allows you to recognize and appreciate their efforts all at once, thus saving you valuable time. Additionally, it strengthens your relationship with the suppliers. Since suppliers see the program from a different perspective, they often have valuable suggestions for improvement that would not come from inside the organization. And because project managers often have to coordinate deliverables or issues between program suppliers, treating them as a team with periodic meetings (typically bimonthly or quarterly) usually results in faster and smoother resolution.

People within a specific skill set, within the program or organization, are also a team. This means, for example, that all of the mechanical engineers within the organization can be viewed and treated as a team. The key to forming teams is that you need enough critical mass in a skill set. If such critical mass does not exist, consider forming a team outside of the program, provided that the organization is large enough. Once again, recognizing a specific skill set as a team creates pride in the skill set, fosters common issues to be raised and resolved, and propagates best practices. In our mechanical engineer example, the engineers may all be doing different things, but part of the team meeting should be a segment during which someone makes a presentation discussing what they do, what their challenges are, and so on.

Unfortunately, the educational system in the United States and some other countries focuses on the individual and working independently, as opposed to as a team, to the point that college graduates are often "team challenged," with a very limited amount of experience working in teams. Combine this with the tendency of some technical types to be introverts, and you can see why the sharing of ideas and best practices across an organization is practically nonexistent in many companies.

A previous Space Shuttle Program (SSP) manager was the first in that position to regularly schedule team meetings for each of the SSP Project Element managers. The SSP Project Element managers are essentially program managers for their areas of responsibility. The team meetings at which the SSP Project Element managers met were called SSP Council meetings. Prior to the council meetings these Project Element managers were already familiar with each other, since they periodically met at formal SSP reviews. However, the council meetings had a more relaxed atmosphere; they were held in nontraditional, desirable locations (locations outside of their regular SSP meetings) and had social activities integrated into the framework of the meeting, and as a result, attendees more openly shared best practices across program elements. This led to a reduction in the adversarial/competitive culture that had existed. Because of the council meetings, everyone began to understand the common challenges they shared, as well as each other's unique challenges.

Know Your Strengths, Weaknesses, and Preferences

When I was planning to form my company for project management training, I sought out a lot of advice. A person who specializes in leadership training told me, "The most important thing in developing the capacity to teach people effectively is the same thing that is required to lead people effectively: that is, you must study and know yourself and be grounded in who you are, because it makes you confident and consistent. This will be very evident to whoever you are teaching or leading."

An important prerequisite for team building and leadership is to "know thyself." Therefore, always take advantage of every opportunity for self-assessment, be it personality profiles or 360-degree feedback studies. Don't discount what the self-assessment tells you. Other people's perception of you, right or wrong, is their reality. Don't be disturbed by your faults, because you are human and everyone has faults. Knowing your faults is critical because it allows you to compensate for or mask the fault in order to minimize the fault's negative impact.

For example, one of my faults is that I am a control freak. I have painfully learned that a solution is not complete unless you have the "buy-in" from the team to implement the solution so I take extra time to achieve buy-in.

Encourage Team Buy-In

Wanting control is a common challenge for the experienced program manager. Realize that already knowing the answer or the plan of attack for a problem is actually a handicap when it comes to establishing team buy-in on the solution or the plan of attack. It may seem expedient to just tell your team the answer, but you must carefully guide them in a way that allows them to find the answer themselves.

To do so, call a meeting, frame the problem you already know the answer to, and let the team find the answer. The solution they propose is then their answer, not yours. Sometimes they may come up with something different, and this is okay, even if you don't consider it optimal. From a developmental perspective, you sometimes have to let your team experience a few bumps and bruises. After all, it is difficult to learn to ride a bike without the occasional fall. Likewise, to build strong teams and strong personnel, the program manager has to accept the occasional failure. Additionally, the program manager who always has time to tell the team what to do is probably ignoring his or her own program management duties.

Handle Failure Positively

This willingness to accept the occasional failure is a critical element in establishing a positive and proactive program culture, and the program manager sets the tone for how the organization handles failures. It is counterproductive to have program personnel make aggressive decisions and then punish them when a poor decision is made. Every organization has an existing culture when it comes to how failures are handled. And unfortunately, a lot of cultures are always looking for the sacrificial lamb, the scapegoat, someone to blame. However, when people are chastised and blamed for poor decisions, they are less likely to make timely decisions in the future and are more unlikely to make aggressive decisions. This contributes to ineffective teams and slows the organization's decision-making processes significantly. As a program manager, you need to liberate your project managers to make aggressive decisions even if they are occasionally wrong.

Acquire Complementary Skills

Preferences often dictate your strengths and weaknesses. That is, we are often weaker in things we don't like. At the program level, you want to make sure that you have people on your team who complement you and who complement each other. Few things are more valuable to the program manager than having capable and trustworthy team members who have complementary skills. This allows you to delegate those responsibilities and tasks that you dislike or are weak in. The program manager has to be strong and confident enough to surround himself or herself with complementary people.

This also means that the team environment will have more turmoil, because there will often be a diversity of opinions or operational preferences. Laurence J. Peter, author of *The Peter Principle*, said, "Only mediocrities rise to the top in a system that won't tolerate wave-making." So be prepared to allow a certain amount of wave-making and "fruitful" discussion. Only insecure program managers try to do everything themselves and/or surround themselves with people who think just like them.

The power of self-assessment is that you can establish a plan to hone your strengths and shore up your weaknesses. Then you can assess your progress over time. Realize that it is very appropriate, especially at the program level, to have a coach. Consider that legendary golfer Tiger Woods has a coach, as do many other top athletes and performers in other fields. Woods also does self-evaluations in order to pinpoint his strengths and make them even stronger.

Create Followership

A strong team is committed to the team goal and the team leader. And when it comes to followership, the "why" question plays an important role. All people are different from one another. Some will follow direction and leadership blindly without having to understand the vision or "why" this is necessary. Others cannot give full effort without understanding the overall vision and why and how the tasks at hand relate to that vision. Therefore, your role is to reiterate the vision, as well as to tell why and how the tasks and current plan relate to that vision. This is a continual effort that has to be performed repeatedly. Additionally, the program manager must make sure that project managers understand the vision and the "why" and relate this information to their project teams.

Program managers are challenged to develop a stable culture in a dynamic and changing environment. The crystal clear communication of program vision is an anchor that helps stabilize the program culture. Never assume that people will remember the vision and the overall purpose of the program, project, or their task. People get so wrapped up in their near-term deliverables and challenges that overall vision and purpose is often forgotten, even when it is a key element of the decision processes that must take place on a daily basis.

When I conduct project management training, I use a project simulation that requires participants to build a bridge. They have to build the bridge under time pressure based on an estimate they created. Once the bridge building begins, they typically become so focused on the tasks that they pay no attention to obvious abnormalities and even get too busy to talk to the customer. This illustrates to the attendees how quickly and easily they can get "head down" and into the task—so much so that they ignore or miss key elements all around them that are or should be impacting the head-down tasks they are working on. The deliverable becomes more important than the purpose.

TIP

Ask people for their verbal commitment to follow your leadership. Ask if they have any concerns with regard to following your leadership. Address any concerns they have and then get their verbal commitment by asking them for it. This is a powerful way to ensure commitment, because psychologists have proven that people have an overwhelming desire to be consistent with their previous actions. The verbal commitment becomes a previous action.

In Robert B. Cialdini's powerful book, *Influence: The Psychology of Persuasion,* he cites consistency as one of the major factors that marketers use to prompt people to make a purchase. For example, you have probably received a sales call or sales presentation in which the salesperson gets you to answer "yes" to a simple or unrelated question. They do this because research shows that if they can get you to say "yes" to anything, no matter how trivial, it becomes more difficult for you to say "no" to a question of substance. Dale Carnegie also illustrates this principle in the book, *How to Win Friends and Influence People.*

So if the "yes" in response to a nonrelated or irrelevant question makes it more difficult for you to say "no," because you will feel inconsistent with your previous yes answers, imagine the power of the eyeball-to-eyeball "yes" answer you get to a request for someone to follow your leadership. Asking for and thanking people for their followership is a powerful way to ensure future commitment, because psychologically it will be difficult for them to be inconsistent with the verbal commitment they have previously made.

Drive Change through Retreats

Retreats can be a very effective team-building tool for program managers. Like any meeting (and a retreat is just a special type of meeting), your retreat needs to have the purpose and the outcomes clearly defined up front. Usually the more planning and forethought that is accomplished prior to the retreat, the better will be the outcomes. Retreats can range from major events with huge budgets to dinner at the program manager's home or favorite restaurant.

One good purpose for a retreat is for the team to get to know each other better. But don't just assume this will happen without some kind of plan or structure. Details can be important, down to seating assignments for activities throughout the retreat. The effectiveness of some retreats is hindered because personnel show up in their natural groups or cliques and stay within those groups for the entire retreat.

TIP

A key element of any retreat or team-building activity is food. Food is a natural ice-breaker and fellowship generator, and it helps relax the team. Deep psychological things happen when you feed people, and as program manager you should feed your team at every opportunity. Bring in bread and bagels in the morning and surprise people with chocolate or popcorn in the afternoon. The results of this small act will amaze you.

Summit Process

You can use a retreat strategically to strengthen teams and address organizational challenges taking advantage of the expertise and experience of the participants. The retreat process can provide a unique window of opportunity for the different parts of the organization to see what everyone else is doing.

> For example, General Michael C. Kostelnik, of the U.S. Air Force was able to accelerate the development of advanced Air Force weapons systems through retreats by using what he defined as a "Summit" process. Typically, the more advanced a weapons system is, the more integration of multiple groups and technology experts is required. The Summit process is very effective for large-scale programs and excels at forcing and structuring this integration so that tangible and actionable plans result. Many of the high-tech weapons used in the Iraq and Gulf wars came out of the Summit process used by the Air Force.

The Summit process starts with the leader clearly defining the goals of the Summit. These goals can include establishing what new products should be developed, how to address specific organizational challenges, or whatever else the program manager sees as the most important challenges or opportunities. The process involves long-term investment of time and energy.

To gain the greatest benefit, the leaders must have an appreciation for the long view and plan the results for use one to two years out. The Summit process itself includes a series of meetings with the kickoff and final "Summit" being large-scale events. It is much more than a retreat because it typically takes place over a six-month to one-year period.

Over the timeframe of the Summit process the organization has had three major meetings: the kickoff, the mid-term, and the Summit itself where the final findings and recommendations are presented. These meetings are more than just get-togethers; they are pacing events that provide opportunities for in-depth discussion, integration with the other teams, and the presentation of the platform by the team leaders. Key elements of the Summit process are as follows.

Pre-Summit

1. Establish the desired outcomes, Summit structure, and panel/team charters.
2. Establish a "chair" (leader) for the Summit.
3. Identify team leaders who are accountable to the chair for each of the major goals and objectives of the Summit.
4. Form cross-functional teams to support team leaders for their goals.

Summit Kickoff

1. The program manager outlines the goal of the Summit and introduces the teams and team leaders.
2. Each team leader presents his or her charter and anticipated deliverables.
3. A schedule for the six-month to one-year process is presented with identification of key milestones and meeting dates.
4. The kickoff meeting has "general sessions" where the preceding is accomplished, including a presentation of the overall Summit schedule. It also includes breakout sessions where the teams agree on their deliverables and establish their internal action plans and methods of operation.
5. Major program stakeholders are invited.

Mid-Term Briefing

1. Team leaders present preliminary findings to the corporate leadership and provide status in general sessions.

2. Breakout sessions for teams are held to both refine the findings and adjust to corporate direction.

3. Goals and objectives of the Summit are adjusted as appropriate.

Final Summit Meeting

1. The program manager reviews the goals, objectives, and process.

2. Team leaders present team reports.

3. The Summit chair gives a summary of results.

4. The program manager gives a plan of action based on outcomes.

5. A final report is issued.

6. There is preplanning of the next Summit.

7. Major program stakeholders are invited.

This process requires organizational commitment of the necessary resources. The process is beneficial, though, because it is a powerful communication tool that ensures the challenges and opportunities of the organization will become known and understood by the entire organization, which is not always true for large-scale programs. Additionally, the use of cross-functional teams to address the challenges encourages "out-of-the-box" thinking that results in breakthroughs or leaps in progress and achievements. Also important is that the Summit process makes justification of changes in program direction easy to sell to stakeholders and the organization. It bolsters the justification of the proposed program budget.

SCENARIO

During the first NASA Summit meeting I attended, I looked at the agenda and thought, "What a waste of time." The agenda was basically forty-five minutes to an hour of presentation or panel session, followed by forty-five minutes of breaks. I later learned through observation and asking around that this is the true power of the Summit process. The breaks are where the "real work" is accomplished. Challenges are presented and then there is opportunity for discussion with participants from across the organization. It is very rare when the "players" of an organization are assembled together and even rarer when they are assembled together and have time for relaxed conversations. The result of this is increased understanding by and of the entire organization about their challenges, and increased trust among organizational members.

It is common in large-scale programs that sublevel program managers or project managers may not fully understand the issues that their peers are facing that have significant ramifications for their own goals and objectives. The program manager always has to be concerned with effective integration, and the Summit process is essentially an integration tool. The Summit process as described is for large programs, but with judgment you can easily adapt or streamline it for smaller programs.

Key Elements of the Summit Process. Key elements of the Summit process that should be considered include the following steps:

- Pick your team leaders carefully. They must have enough status in the organization to be able to draw upon all of its resources, but not be so consumed with day-to-day work that they can't break away for substantive working meetings outside of the three meetings previously addressed.
- Hold the Summit meetings in venues where people can golf or enjoy other recreational activities, and the hotel has amenities suitable for "structured fun" evening gatherings.
- Have extended breaks during the meetings.
- Have tangible objectives with cross-functional teams. The objectives are typically outside the scope of normal activities and responsibilities.
- Have someone assigned to manage the process, track actions and create an overall schedule.

Use Performance Appraisals in Program Management

Fundamentally, people behave according to how they are rewarded. A major element in the formal organizational process that impacts how people are rewarded is the performance appraisal system. Most mature or reasonably mature organizations have a formalized system for performance appraisals. The program manager should understand all the "ins and outs" of the performance appraisal system in order to maximize the ability to reward top performers, as well as to help improve or remove marginal performers from the project team.

Knowing the ins and outs also means having relationship capital with all the gatekeepers and decision makers in the performance appraisal process. Like any bureaucratic process, there are rules and then there is what you can really do. Often the decision makers and the gatekeepers can help you do what you want to do more appropriately, which is reward performance, versus what the "institutionalized performance appraisal process" supposedly allows you to do.

It is the program manager's prerogative to do everything possible to reward the best-performing program personnel. Unfortunately, many good program managers get caught up in the day-to-day challenges of the program and forget about the program personnel. However, you must take care of the people first. Once you do, everything else tends to take care of itself.

Provide Positive Reinforcement

Usually at the program level, the program manager is mature and secure in his or her abilities and needs little if any reinforcement from others. Because of this, program managers often discount the importance that program personnel place on the performance appraisal process and other things program managers may view as trivial. But program personnel who may be less experienced and/or secure need constant reinforcement. Therefore, the program manager needs to assess how much influence or control the performance appraisal process has over program personnel. The amount of influence may vary because of organizational or program structure.

The program manager should also have a strategy for exerting influence over personnel whose performance appraisals he or she does not perform. This strategy can include letters to the responsible person who does the performance appraisal. You can then state it as program policy that all "in house" company or organizational personnel will get periodic letters documenting their performance and contribution to the program. Periodic can mean quarterly, at the major milestones, at key deliverables for the supporting personnel, or just prior to the creation of performance evaluations.

Create Leverage outside the Program Structure

Additionally, the program manager can seek and gain approval to be formally included in the performance appraisal process for key program personnel that are outside of the program structure. It may also be beneficial to allow outside input for project managers who support the outside organizations. If the program has a project manager supporting the marketing organization, then marketing has a right to make an input on that project managers performance and the program manager should seek that input. The intent of this type of power sharing is to drive positive performance in the direction of the ultimate customer, so that they will be able to view your performance from their own perspective. Often our zeal to complete all of the many tasks on our plate, combined with organizational pressure and change, may cause us to stray from the customer service perspective.

Ultimately, the performance appraisal system should foster teamwork. This means that the program manager should ensure that the performance plan and goals include criteria that rate the project manager's effectiveness at building teams and being a team member.

Judge the Strength of Followership

While there are many different styles, strategies, and tactics of leadership, a necessary result of good leadership is the strength of your followership. Do people follow you because of your title only? Because of your professional reputation? Technical skills? Trustworthiness? Consistency? It may be because of all or some of the above, but if trustworthiness and consistency are lacking, your followership is weak. As the program manager, you must remember that everyone judges your every action and statement for trustworthiness and trustworthiness creates *followership*.

Use Recognition Activities for Individuals and Teams

Both individuals and teams need to be recognized. Realize, though, that recognition is a two-edged sword and has as much or more potential to demotivate and weaken a team as it does to build up a team. A quick compliment sometimes seems appropriate, but if the wrong person is given the praise or if the praise is given to one person when multiple people were involved, the praise can hurt the team. Therefore, always praise the team first. This is especially true for public praise. Make sure you have done your homework and are complimenting the right person for the right circumstance. Personal praise is best done in private "one-on-one" where there's little potential for negative impact on the team. Only offer individual praise in a group setting if there is a strategic or compelling reason for doing so.

The program manager should also counsel project managers, and other direct reports to always publicly share praise with the team whenever they receive it. Only a poor or uninformed leader accepts kudos without immediately complimenting his or her team. Also note that the exact opposite holds true for criticism. Uninformed leaders place blame on their team when receiving criticism, while the strong leader accepts criticism without deflecting it to others, even when it is not his or her fault. The leader's role is to build up the team by passing on compliments, and to maintain integrity by accepting all criticism for the team. Both of the aforementioned build loyalty and followership and should be taught to project managers by program managers through words and deeds.

Tell your project team that as program manager you may receive recognition more frequently. Also tell them that as project managers they may receive special recognition more frequently than the team does. If the recognition is significant and/or lends itself to it, you can turn almost any individual achievement into a team recognition event by having a "Thank you; I couldn't have done it without you" party. Always try to turn recognition activities into team-building activities.

TIP

Don't discount that people like to be recognized and complimented. Here is a simple experiment to verify this. The next time you are around a three- to five-year-old child, observe the child's behavior. When she does something well, look her in the eye and give her some praise and recognition. You will see her face and whole body "light up" in response to the praise. Praise is that powerful. The only difference in the response of a three- to five-year-old and your team to praise is that as adults we have been trained to hide our glee with a simple "thank you." But hidden on the inside is the same powerful effect you see in the three- to five-year-old child. No wonder Mark Twain wrote: "I can live two months on a good compliment." Be on the lookout for praise opportunities, including examination of program metrics that may show sustained good performance or improving performance. Either condition is a praise opportunity to take advantage of.

The power of praise is often amplified depending upon what level of the power structure the praise comes from. In other words, praise from the vice president may carry more weight than praise from the project manager. As a program manager, you can leverage this fact. That is, on occasion, you can write letters and award nominations to be signed and/or presented by high-level leaders to program personnel. The key is to make it easy and seamless for the high-level leader by providing the words or writing the note for him. This is especially effective when you can write it in his or her voice (her secretary or assistant can help with this). Doing this also provides some good exposure of the work of your top performing personnel (individuals and teams).

More important than all the recognition you can personally give is training your team to frequently use with each other on a regular basis the two most important recognition words in the English language. Those words are "thank you." We often get so caught up in the daily pressures of work that the common courtesy of a sincere thank-you is an afterthought. Does your organization have a culture in which people thank each other regularly, or do you have an "it's their job" culture and no thanks are necessary? As a program manager, you lead by example when it comes to thanking others and establishing a positive culture.

One tactic you can easily deploy and that works well is to ask the following question at the beginning or the end of a meeting: "Is there anyone who would like to thank someone else for a good job this week or for going above and beyond the call of duty?" This one question gets your team in the habit of thanking each other and takes the pressure off of you as the leader to always be the one to recognize good work. As you ask this question over a period of time, the act of publicly thanking people soon becomes habit for your team. More important, in work environments where people appreciate each other regularly, the occasional inconsiderate act is often overlooked or easily forgiven.

The first time you use this technique, don't expect everyone to talk at once. The good news is that you can "prime the pump," since you know you are going to ask someone to thank someone else. Before the meeting, approach one of your most trusted personnel and tell him or her to thank one or two people if she sees no one responding to your question. This is usually enough to break the ice and get the ball rolling. After several meetings it becomes a natural part of the process and has a way of migrating way past the meeting setting.

Another weapon in the program manager's arsenal for recognition is the handwritten note—not an e-mail, not a preprinted thank-you card, but a handwritten note. This means ink on paper in your distinctive handwriting. You should have within arm's distance of your work environment and in your briefcase assorted blank thank-you cards. Handwritten notes go a long way because they show that you value the recipient enough to take your personal time to acknowledge his or her contribution or effort.

Many program managers don't write thank-you notes because they don't know what to write. If you fall in this category, I suggest you get a copy of *Effective Phrases for Performance Appraisals* by James E. Neal. It is filled with sentence chunks for every trait (positive and negative) that any employee can have. You simply find the trait the person exhibited that you wish to compliment or highlight, copy it, and you have a nice thank-you card in minutes. This book is equally helpful for performance appraisals, letters of recommendation, award nominations, etc. No one is going to give you a medal for struggling to write all the words yourself.

Deal with Breaches of Program Integrity and Ethics

When you work with and lead human beings, occasionally you will have breaches of program integrity and/or ethics. The more people you work with and lead, the more this "occasionally" seems to surface. Often the violation is a result of a complete lack of judgment or complete willful intent that makes you and others wonder: "What were they thinking or drinking?" The program manager often has to address these violations, which can range from skipping or falsifying process steps to taking kickbacks or "special favors" from contractors.

When dealing with any type of violation, you want to investigate, expose, and then intercede. When you investigate, you want to make sure you separate the facts from the fiction that often surrounds these circumstances. Their violation may have just been because of an oversight or misunderstanding. Depending on the nature of the infraction, it may be best to use an internal or external auditor. Weigh this decision carefully, as what the auditor uncovers is not easily recovered.

This leads to an expose. By expose I don't mean exposing the circumstance to everyone. I mean making a conscious decision about how much exposure is beneficial to the program and/or has to be morally or legally made known. Just because something happened or something is true doesn't mean everyone needs to know it. The amount of exposure to give an incident should be planned and controlled.

Interceding means taking the necessary corrective action to eliminate or minimize the impact of the occurrence and reduce the likelihood of future occurrences. Hopefully you have fostered an environment of teamwork and trust. Trust violations may sometimes be handled by the team, but they will usually expect you to address them, and you should. A breach of integrity and ethics is a trust violation and a threat to the fabric of your team and your leadership. Ultimately, when not properly addressed, such violations reflect negatively on you and the program.

People who prove themselves untrustworthy should be given a second chance. However, you shouldn't feel obligated to be the one to give it to them. Once you have a documented violation, you need to discreetly recheck the person's current reputation, actions, and history for clues, trends, or previous wrongdoing. Start thinking, planning, and executing the steps to get the person to a "happier place." A happier place may be defined as "not in your program," since you are no longer happy with the person.

If you can't move the person to a happier place in a reasonable amount of time, you may have to start freezing the individual out of critical discussions and assignments. Every situation is different, and you have to use judgment. However, people who prove themselves untrustworthy or divisive tend to prove it over and over. Your job is to protect the program and the other team members from these types of people.

As a program manager, you'll spend a substantial portion of your time building strong teams and ensuring that leaders within the program are building strong teams. The strength of any team is ultimately tested by how they respond to challenges, whether "real-time" or entrenched organizational problems. Program managers who build strong teams are investing in the organization's future. As such, team building is an important part of program culture and should be planned like any other program activity.

KEYSTONES

Team Building at the Program Level

1. The program manager needs to think about all the possible teams, internal and external to the program.
2. To lead teams effectively you must study and know yourself and be grounded in who you are.
3. Building strong teams and strong personnel means the program manager has to accept the occasional failure.

4. The program manager's continual role is to reiterate the vision, as well as why and how tasks and current plans relate to that vision.

5. Asking for and thanking people for their followership is a powerful way to ensure future commitment.

6. Retreats can be a very effective team-building tool for the program manager.

7. The Summit process involves a series of organized retreats that excels at forcing and structuring integration so tangible and actionable plans result.

8. As program manager you must take care of people first and then everything else tends to take care of itself.

9. Individuals and teams need regular praise.

10. When a breach of program integrity occurs you must investigate, prudently expose, and then intercede.

Program Communication Processes

All program managers need to strategically choose program communication processes. Unfortunately, technology has complicated the decision-making process for the program manager, providing a myriad of available choices for means for communication. Because there are so many choices, confusion often results. Our ability to extract the value out of technological advances in communication methods lags by the rate at which new methods are created.

Notifiership

A second-career program manager (who retired as program manager for one company and came out of retirement for another company) confided in me that he believed his organization would perform better program management without the desktop—without any of the automated project management tools on the market today. He further stated that too many people think the tool is the solution—that the tool will solve all the communication problems and virtually run the project as if it is on cruise control. His point was that he thinks many project managers today have become bean counters rather than implementers of the project. As such, the bean-counting project managers rely on the tool to send automated e-mail messages to team members informing them that a task is behind schedule or completed.

Notifiership has replaced leadership. He recalled the days when people would go into a project "war room" with hand-drawn or magnetic schedules on the wall, and the entire project team would meet to resolve issues "face-to-face" with everyone talking about the same thing at the same time.

The odds that the desktop with all of its capabilities is going away are nil, but what he misses from "predesktop" days is focused face-to-face communication. I agree with his point that many project managers have become bean counters rather than implementers. However, today's world of virtual and global teams requires successful communication strategies, even when face-to-face communication is minimal or impossible. This situation is not an excuse for notifiership. Effective project management requires more than sending e-mails "notifying" people of their responsibility. Project management teams need to be led even when they are virtual or global. Therefore, program managers must ensure that project managers use communication methods to lead teams and that they don't fall into the notifiership habit. Communication processes are leadership processes.

Focused face-to-face communication is still an element that is used for successful program management even in virtual and global teams; therefore, it must be accounted for and built into the program culture. Overall, communication can be either written or personal. Written communication can be paper, such as a handwritten note or printed memo, or electronic, such as instant messages, e-mails, or Web based. Personal communication can be face-to-face or electronic. Personal electronic communication can be audio or video (live or taped). The opportunity for face-to-face communication can be a precious one; therefore, you need to leverage it in order to have the maximum impact on the program. Schedule face-to-face meetings at important program junctures and to establish the foundation of relationships for program success. The more remote the team, the more face-to-face communication opportunities are valued.

Program Meetings

The program manager should define a structure, rules, and guidelines for all program meetings. Periodically the program manager should examine all the regularly scheduled meetings within the program to see if there are efficiencies or gaps. In today's business and program environment, you would be hard-pressed to identify a bigger consumer or waster of organizational resources than meetings. The fact is that a lot of meetings are unnecessary, and often the necessary meetings are poorly run.

How well a program manager's project managers run and execute meetings is a reflection of the program manager and the program itself. The program manager should let project managers know that he or she may occasionally sit in on their project meetings to maintain a feel for what's going on in the program. Periodically doing this not only provides the program manager an improved feel for the program, but also ensures that meetings are being conducted properly and efficiently. If the program manager senses they are not, then he or she must take action immediately. Adherence to

Roberts Rules of Order for conducting meetings is usually not necessary, but organization and discipline in meetings are required.

In the Project Management Leadership classes I conduct, I often ask the class: "Has anyone in this class ever traveled through time?" While I receive a few puzzled looks from that question, I never get a raised hand. I then say: "You probably have traveled through time; you just never realized it. If I could step into one of your organization's meetings, and the same people are making the same points about the same issue they discussed six months ago, all while drinking out of the same coffee cup they did six months ago, then you have traveled through time."

Talking about the same issues ad nauseam is a symptom of poor meetings and decision processes, and is a major contributor to déjà vu and the perception of time travel. A meeting is a key element in the process of how a project team, a program, and an organization make decisions. However, poorly run meetings are a major source of frustration and a contributor to apathy. You can minimize the effects of poorly run meetings by adhering to the following guidelines.

1. Be clear about the purpose of the meeting. People should always know why they are coming and what are the anticipated outcomes for the meeting.

2. Have a complete agenda. Complete means it identifies all the items that will be discussed with time estimates for each item, and the items are in priority order. The agenda should clearly indicate the decisions that need to be made. A good agenda is also issued ahead of time and can require "prework" for meeting participants. Prework can be anything that saves time at the meeting by having it completed before the meeting. For example, a prework statement may be: "Come to the meeting with seven ideas on how we can improve customer satisfaction." Even if

people forget or don't bring the requested prework (and some will), they have still been asked the question and their subconscious mind will have been thinking about the item, thus resulting in more fruitful discussions at the meeting.

3. At the meeting, make sure people follow the agenda. Enforcing this at the program level frees and encourages project managers to do it at their level. If the program manager runs sloppy meetings, so will the project managers. How meetings are run is often an organizational culture issue that is reflective of the leadership. Tell your project managers and program personnel that they do not have to and should not stay in meetings that don't have an agenda, and that if they get push-back, they should tell the person chairing the meeting to call you. Telling them this is in effect also telling them not to have any meetings without an agenda.

4. Do not let one person dominate the meeting or agenda. Others will blame you for a lack of control at a meeting. People who like to unfairly or haphazardly dominate meetings are usually known or show themselves early.

5. Do not let unnecessary people crash your meeting. In some companies or very large programs, there are certain people who go to meetings just to "see what's going on." There may be nothing inherently wrong with this, but often in meetings more people can lead to less progress. Before a meeting, you can ask each person what his or her purpose is for being at the meeting. If someone's purpose is not grounded, then politely ask that person to leave.

6. Start and end the meeting on time. This shows respect for everyone's time and is indicative of a well-construed and well-organized meeting.

7. Use time pressure during meetings. In some meetings, 80 percent of the progress happens in the 20 percent of time before you lose the conference room. Sometimes having more time isn't the answer and having a deadline is. Time pressure can be a good thing at meetings because it forces focus. Having "stand-up" meetings without chairs is an effective and commonly deployed tactic for creating more efficient meetings. It works especially well for a "fifteen minute" start-the-day status meeting for project teams.

8. Use odd start times to help people remember the meeting time. For instance, start your meeting at 1:07 p.m. Seven minutes is odd, and it also provides a window of time for people who were in a meeting that ended at 1:00 p.m. to arrive on time at your meeting.

9. Lock in points of agreement. Meeting discussions, especially planning-meeting discussions, often wander for a while before the group settles on a decision, finding, or course of action. The meeting chair needs to always be on the lookout for these points and to take time out to confirm, in a round-robin fashion, that all individuals are in agreement. This locks in the agreement of the entire group. It is okay for someone to disagree or dissent. Acknowledge the disagreement, address it if needed, and then move to agreement. Locking in points of agreement is important for two reasons:

   • A lot of time is often wasted in meetings discussing something everyone agrees to.
   • The agreement needs to be sealed so that people don't go back and discuss it again. Seeking verbal commitment and agreement invokes the psychological rule of consistency, and people will consider carefully before going back on their verbal commitment. This keeps the meeting from going in circles.

10. Record meeting outcomes. These can include minutes, action items, assignments, and whatever else needs to be documented and tracked. The advent of technology means that meetings can be digitally recorded with a microrecorder, provided the organizational culture and team allows it. You can then transcribe the recording as necessary. When you're working with multiple suppliers and organizations, creating audio and video recordings of design reviews and other major milestones provides a concrete record of the event and helps drive accountability.
11. Religiously follow up on action items.

E-mail Guidelines

Just like in advertising, the most important part of an e-mail is the title or subject line. The title communicates what the e-mail is about, and it may be one of hundreds the recipient has in his or her inbox. Your team's productivity can increase dramatically if you establish a common title structure.

For example, if an e-mail is an action item, the title should be labeled ACTION. It is very frustrating to find out you have an action item in an e-mail that is clandestinely embedded in the message's third paragraph. Likewise, if the e-mail is information only, it could be labeled INFO ONLY, or READ IMMED for read immediately. Standard titles tell the recipient what is required of them before they open the e-mail. Whatever title you choose, remember that e-mails should only address one single topic area. This simplifies the management and informal tracking of e-mails for both the sender and recipient.

Program participants should remember and be reminded that e-mail is a public communication method. If you are not willing to say it publicly, e-mail is not the communication method to use.

Not only can e-mail be read by an internal IT administrator, but under certain legal circumstances e-mails can become a matter of public record. E-mails are not private or secure. Along those lines you must consider the political ramifications of what is written in an e-mail if it is forwarded or copied to an unintended recipient. Also, from a political perspective, you need to be mindful of including names in e-mails, especially with regard to behavior or performance issues. Consideration also needs to be given to personnel when e-mailing outside the program structure, especially with regard to making organizational commitments or promises to the customer.

If you are sending an e-mail to one person and it is an item of significance, a phone call or personal visit may be more appropriate. If an e-mail is going to multiple personnel, and if there are separate actions or requirements for each recipient, they should be delineated specifically by name so it is crystal clear who is expected to do what. When you receive an e-mail and it requires a response (not information only), reply within twenty-four hours, even if the response just promises when you will respond with the answer.

In general, e-mails should be short. If the text exceeds a page view, consider putting the detailed text in an attachment. When an e-mail length exceeds a page view, most readers scan the message rather than actually read it. Additionally, short paragraphs are easier to read.

Never use all caps when writing an e-mail message. Because it is a "colder" method of communication, e-mail often comes across harsher than verbalized words. Therefore, always be polite in your messages by including hello greetings, thank yous, regards, etc. And always include your contact information at the bottom of an e-mail. Finally, if you expect the recipient to take some sort of action, be explicit about what you want the person to do.

Many people attempt to use e-mail as a documentation trail. There is nothing inherently wrong with that, but if that's your intent, then be clear and upfront about it in the e-mail. Also give thought to who really needs to be cc'd on an e-mail. Some people blindly cc everyone.

E-mails are another reflection of a program's image and a vital part of a program's communications processes. Because they are such an important part of the program culture, they need to be managed appropriately.

Team Charters

The team charter is a very important communications tool, as its goal is to eliminate miscommunications that are rooted in false assumptions by establishing a framework of agreement for team interactions. For example, some team members may expect decisions to be established by consensus, while others may expect the leader to decide. Such false assumptions will contribute to resentment when the assumption is found to be untrue. Realize that false does not mean incorrect or wrong as much as it means different from someone else's. Humans have a propensity to believe and think that everyone believes and thinks like they do. However, if a team has six members, the probability that all of them will bring the same set of assumptions and rules to the table is slim. The impact of false assumptions is amplified when the team is culturally diverse.

The team charter minimizes resentment and animosity by defining the "rules of engagement" for the team upfront. It does this by normalizing expectations for the team. Having written agreement on team behavior also provides the team the opportunity and responsibility to self-regulate, meaning that the team will fix most of their problems before the leader has to get involved. Once the charter is developed and agreed on by the team members, all the team members sign the charter. Signing the charter creates psychological pressure to comply with the elements of the charter. Please note that the team charter is not a project charter, although at the discretion of the project manager it could be a subset of the project charter.

DOCUMENT
Key Elements of a Team Charter

1. *Decision Processes*—How will the team make decisions? Will the team use consensus decision making? Will the team use democracy as a decision-making method? Or will the team leader make the decisions after hearing input from all the team members? My personal preference (as a control freak) is the latter. Democracy and consensus can be risky because everyone does not bring the same level of experience to the table. Realize, though, that the method of the team leader making decisions works only when the leader genuinely listens to all team members and is not applicable to all cultures. You can't fake listening, and each team member must have the opportunity to speak and be heard. Whatever decision processes the team decides to use, you need to document it in the charter and obtain buy-in from the team.

2. *Meetings*—Details of how meetings should be conducted are discussed elsewhere in this chapter. From the perspective of the team charter, the following points should be defined:

   - Are meetings going to start on time or start late? One of the unpleasant disorders many organizations suffer from is meetings that never start on time, with people arriving at the meetings 10 to 30 minutes after the scheduled start time. This becomes frustrating to the people who are on time. When this issue is not corrected, eventually everyone knows the meeting won't start until 15 to 20 minutes after it was scheduled to start, so no one arrives on time. This becomes a contributing factor to a dysfunctional team, because time is wasted and meetings become unproductive. Usually the team members will fault the leader for not having control of the team, and they will bear silent resentment.

   - The team charter becomes a mechanism that can improve this situation. When constructing the team charter with the team, the leader says: "Let's decide as a team whether we are going to be on time for meetings or fashionably late to the meetings." If the team decides they are committing to being on time, that's great. You can then ask what the penalty is for being late. Decide on this penalty as a team. Some teams assess a dollar or two, which is kept in a kitty until it is enough to sponsor a team party or donate to a charity of the team's choice. Or the penalty could be that the person has to bring snacks or drinks to the next meeting.

- If the team decides they can't commit to being on time for meetings, then determine how long will be the grace period for being late. Will it be five minutes? Ten minutes? Fifteen minutes? Does the person have to call the meeting chair and advise that he or she will be late? Does the person have to send a capable replacement to act on her behalf if she is unable to attend the meeting? Is the team empowered to make decisions in the absence of a team member? This should be agreed upon by the team in the charter.

3. *E-mail*—This chapter has a section on how e-mail can be used. The team's method of choice for e-mail use can be defined here. In some work environments, it is a good idea to document that only work-related e-mails are allowed in order to minimize internal spam.

4. *Conflict Resolution*—The process for resolving conflicts within the team should be defined upfront, and the team charter is a good place to document this process. Conflicts are a natural part of any work environment. Fortunately, most conflicts are and can be resolved within the team. There may be rare occasions when conflicts cannot be resolved internal to the team. Defining the conflict resolution process ahead of time, including the steps to escalate unresolved conflicts, often reduces resentment and actually helps resolve conflicts quicker. Team members will often not want the conflict escalated to higher levels of leadership as the process requires and will work harder for internal resolution. This process reduces resentment because if it did not exist and a conflict had to be escalated by the team leader, the team members and possibly others would say: "She didn't have to take that to the VP or CIO." When you establish this rule you need to let the leader to whom the escalated issues will be brought know that he is part of the process and get his agreement. The program manager should also let project managers know that their unresolved project issues can be brought to them.

5. *Crisis Management*—The team charter can predefine how crises will be handled. Will one person contact everyone? Or will a calling chain be

established? In every company and program, things happen, such as blackouts, winter storms, hurricanes, or even injury to fellow team members. How this news reaches the team, and the corresponding actions the team should follow, must be predefined. Doing so ensures that the team stays on track (or goes off track very little) no matter what happens.

6. *Feedback Processes*—The team charter can assure that the team leader and team members will give each other verbal feedback at every major milestone or every two months (or appropriate time period) in the absence of a major milestone.

7. *After-Hours Communication*—In today's technologically driven environment we have twenty-four-hour access to communication methods. This has blurred and sometimes erased the lines between when someone is "at work" and is "not at work." Therefore, the team leader should establish criteria for the team that defines when a team member is not at work. I personally believe in maintaining life balance, and for my teams that means I am only contacted during nonwork hours when (1) the building is on fire, or (2) the VP or CIO has personally requested to see me. Some program personnel are what you might call "high maintenance"— that is, they call other program team members any time of the day about trivial matters. Having a team charter minimizes this kind of behavior.

   The need for after-hours communications in the team charter becomes more critical in global operations across time zones because the window of opportunity during which all team members can communicate with one another within their respective normal working hours is limited. The team leader needs to make sure the team is respectful of the working hours for personnel in other time zones, as this promotes a more productive program management culture.

   All personnel deserve some work/life balance. Consistently working people long hours at the expense of a balanced family life is detrimental to the individual and the program over the long term. Errors, omissions, and lack of creative thinking all result when people haven't had proper rest. That's why there are laws limiting how long people who support or operate public transportation systems can work on the job. When people are overworked, they are more prone to making costly and even devastating mistakes. Not overworking personnel requires discipline that begins at the program level.

8. *Professionalism*—A lack of professional demeanor can be detrimental to a team because it can cause resentment and lack of respect for the leader when it is allowed to persist. People will perceive the leader as

"not in control." The team charter can reduce a lot of these types of issues. Raising voices, cursing, and not treating people with respect are all detrimental to the team. If necessary, dress code can be included in this list, especially for personnel interacting with the customer.

9. *Personnel Turnover*—What will the team do in the event that a team member leaves? People do get transferred, relocated, or sick on occasion. The team charter paves the way for sharing the additional workload resulting from the loss of a team member, if team members agree. In the absence of this agreement, when a team member is lost, other team members seem to "disappear," making it more difficult for the team leader to reallocate work activities.

Periodically review the team charter to ensure its validity and for improvement opportunities. A lot of the things the team charter addresses should not have to be addressed in a professional work environment, but unfortunately the charter will demonstrate its value tremendously when these circumstances arise and they will.

The charter may be extended to include other things to foster teamwork, including things like "the last Friday of the month is Hawaiian shirt day," or "The first Tuesday of each month the team will meet for breakfast," or "Birthdays in each month will be celebrated and whoever has a birthday in that month must bring the cake or the dessert." The charter can be used to incorporate any team-building activities the team buys into. Here is an example of a team charter:

DOCUMENT

Blue Beard Team Charter Example

1. We will be on time for meetings with a five-minute grace period.
2. Any team member who is late or an unplanned "no-show" will pay a $2 penalty that will be given to the United Way.
3. If we are unable to attend the meeting or will not arrive within the grace period, we will notify the meeting chair.
4. If my schedule does not allow me to attend a meeting, I will send a capable person to act on my behalf or empower the team to make team decisions in that meeting without me.

5. When sending e-mails to team members, the title will identify if it is an ACTION, NEEDS TO BE READ IMMEDIATELY, or INFORMATION ONLY.

6. Team members agree to send only work-related e-mails to the entire team.

7. Team members agree that if there is a conflict we cannot resolve internally, then that conflict will first be escalated to the program manager and then to the VP of operations.

8. In the event of a crisis, the team leader and/or a designated backup for the team leader will contact everyone on the team with the latest crisis information and the team's planned response, if any.

9. The team members will give one another feedback on performance within two weeks of every major milestone or every two months in the absence of major milestones,

10. The team will contact each other after normal working hours only in the case of an emergency. (An "emergency" can be defined in the charter and may include project or operational issues at the team's discretion.)

11. The team agrees to treat everyone with respect at all times and will not yell or curse at one another and will not speak negatively of others when they are not present.

Virtual and Global Teams

A significant challenge for program managers is leading virtual and/or global teams. Today, technology and multinational corporations are making the virtual or global team common. A virtual team is more demanding to lead because of the communication challenges that arise from personnel being dispersed and not having regular or any access to face-to-face communication. Leading a virtual or global team is even more challenging when the team includes members from different cultures. Although cost savings sometimes is the driving force behind virtual teams, they do require more money and time to manage successfully. The program manager needs to take this into account during the planning process.

Wherever I speak or teach, project managers are all looking for the magic bullets for working globally successfully. I highly recommend the book by Charles Hampden-Turner and Fons Trompenaars, *Managing People across Cultures*. However, when it comes to global teams you will never be able to read it all in a book or get it all in a training class.

Identify a Culture Coach

Leading culturally diverse teams is more than just leading people from countries that have different cultures. There are different cultures within industries, professions, companies, and then within the organizations of those countries. Within the individual organization, there often exist subcultures as well. So in order to be successful, you need to manage a wide spectrum of cultures. This spectrum is so varied that it just can't be covered in a book or training class at the level of effectiveness necessary for success.

A leading global company provides its program managers a coach on the culture of the company—someone in the organization who can coach the program manager on the culture and provide perspective and history on what works and what doesn't. The coach doesn't have to be at a high level in the organization; he or she just has to understand the organization. The coach can help you quickly find the "norms" within the organization that serve as grounding points. You may eventually find these norms without a coach, but the coach accelerates the process and minimizes costly mistakes.

In addition to a coach, there are two key elements to success with virtual and global teams.

1. Have an open mind and be willing to adjust as the circumstances provide you feedback. The best sport's coaches adjust their tactics to the circumstances of the game. Be ready to adjust.

2. Be ready to learn a lot from other cultures. One culture doesn't always have the right answer or the best way to do something. Leading global teams can be an opportunity to leverage the things you have learned from the spectrum of cultures you are working with if you are looking for those things. When you encounter differences, assess the pluses and minuses of the differences and what you can do to migrate the advantages to other parts of the organization or the program.

Be Aware of Potential Communication Issues

The most difficult part of the virtual team is in the area of communication, specifically the lack of that informal communication that results from the trust generated by face-to-face proximity. In virtual and global teams, the hallway conversation doesn't exist. E-mail becomes the lifeblood of communication, but it can become so voluminous that it's more a hindrance than a help. Identifying problems in the virtual environment becomes more difficult, especially if you have people playing politics for whatever reason.

When working virtually or globally, you need to meet face-to-face as many people on the team as you can. This should be done as much as possible and should be budgeted for. Informal dinners with team members are invaluable. Much of what is accomplished in the virtual team environment still happens because of relationships (leadership not notifiership). So it should go without saying that clear goals, roles, and responsibilities are necessary, and after this there is no substitute for the face-to-face meeting, especially at key program and project junctures.

People tend to forgive or give the benefit of the doubt to people they physically work with every day when something is late, imperfect, or not as expected. They see firsthand the demanding circumstances their coworker is in and thus are more understanding.

But on remote teams without any face-to-face meetings, people know each other only by their execution. When that fails or is not perfect, resolving the situation becomes more problematic. People are less understanding and become more critical. Remind your teams of the necessity of not being overly critical of remote team members and of making an extra effort to understand the root cause when there is a problem or delay.

Given the dynamics of virtual teaming, the more things you can standardize, the smoother the team will function. Establishing a weekly status meeting goes a long way toward establishing positive communications. Realize that the status meeting goes both ways—that project and program personnel are looking for information from the program manager. In addition to extracting information from the project managers and team members, the program manager has to provide information that defines the status of the overall program. In global teams, meeting times should also be set or rotated so that one person or portion of the team is not always inconvenienced by having to meet after hours.

Use Varied Communication Tools. Tools also facilitate communication. The capability of Web-conferencing tools continues to evolve. These tools now have the ability to allow participants to vote and to enable anyone participating in a Web conference to mark up the document under discussion or review. These are valuable features that foster good communication in the meeting. Additionally, having the ability to instant message members of a virtual team helps create community and can reduce burdensome e-mail traffic. You can also provide an open conference call line that permits members to communicate with each other at a moment's notice.

The program manager has to consider all aspects of tools and processes that can enable a successful culture in the virtual environment. Personnel should be trained on whatever communication technologies that will be used, even if it is considered fundamental. People are often reluctant to admit they don't understand or know how to use basic tools, and the virtual environment makes them less likely to ask.

As program manager you must hold project managers accountable for good communication in the virtual environment. Saying that you told or notified someone doesn't relieve the program manager of the responsibility of ensuring understanding among team members.

Finally, the program manager should carefully select members of remote teams. The size of the team is important, as smaller teams will bond quicker and often work more effectively. Additionally, competence and being a self-starter is more important for remote team members. Remote team members should have the maturity of knowing when to seek help and to ask the right questions. Over the longer term, it benefits the program manager to plan new virtual teams with personnel who have worked together virtually before. The program manager has to look beyond the current task, deliverable, or project and build strong virtual teams that provide dividends for the life of the program. This is an organizational capability that should be grown over time. Over a period of months and years this becomes very powerful and should be a major consideration in determining how assignments are made for virtual and global teams.

Program Presentation Basics

How the program manager and program personnel make presentations is a reflection of the program's credibility and effectiveness. Therefore, the program manager has to ensure that all program presentations are professional and meet the needs of the decision maker and/or audience for the presentation.

The following principles will help ensure good presentations for the program:

1. *Know the objective for the presentation.* You should know what the presentation is supposed to accomplish. Is it a presentation to inform? Is a decision required? Whatever the goal, the presentation should be structured to maximize achievement of that goal. Additionally, the program manager needs to make sure that the person giving the presentation also knows the goals and objectives.

2. *Know the audience or decision maker.* Know their preferences, likes, and dislikes with regard to how they receive information. You then structure the presentation in the manner that best fits the decision maker's personal style. Some decision makers like lots of background information, framing, and buildup before the issue is discussed. Others want the issue presented immediately and will ask for additional information if they deem it relevant. Some like fancy charts and graphics, while others may want an across-the-table discussion with no paper. Whatever the preference, you must know it, especially for high-level decision makers.

The organization's political environment is dynamic, and high-level organizational leaders and stakeholders often change. Don't assume that the preferences of the new leader are the same as those of the previous leader.

SCENARIO

For example, I am aware of an organization that got a new CEO. At the first briefing for the CEO, executives presented him with a detailed organizational history going back a decade or more. Halfway into the first presentation, the new CEO said, "I don't need to know all of that history right now. I just want to know what your top ten problems are." The executives were not properly prepared to address this.

It was no surprise to the executives that the new CEO was coming. They had prepared for weeks for the presentations, yet none of the executive staff had done adequate research to find out how he liked his information. The fact that he was a "top ten problems" kind of guy should have been easy to uncover. His past and current secretaries, assistants, and direct reports could have revealed that information, but no one bothered to ask. At the very least, you can always ask the person directly: "I want to maximize the use of your time. Do you have any preferences in how I bring information to you?"

TIP

Sometimes it is advantageous to "pre-brief" your decision maker or provide him or her with a cheat sheet. In the chapter on stakeholder management we talked about cheat sheets. The term "cheat sheet" implies that it is an informal method of communication. As stated before, a cheat sheet should be short and used judiciously. It often has a higher chance of getting read than an e-mail, especially for certain types of leaders.

3. *Know your material.* There is no excuse for the program managers or project manager to be inadequately prepared for a presentation. If you're not ready to present for some reason, it is always better to reschedule than to try to present without sufficient preparation. I have seen good presentations launch careers and bad presentations ruin them. In addition to knowing your material, you must be able to look confident at the presentation, as confidence conveys success. Always have your project managers do formal dry runs with you to ensure they are ready to present. Additionally, this will help build their confidence.

You never want your project managers to stumble during the presentation. I mean stumble in such a way that shows they are unprepared for whatever reason. Unfortunately, once an audience sees a stumble or a point of weakness, suddenly everyone seems to have a question. People who were half asleep are now at full attention pondering questions they can ask.

My Ph.D. dissertation advisor provided me with some valuable wisdom on this topic that has served me well over the years. He told me that for every presentation, always brainstorm the ten hardest questions someone can ask you and write out the answers ahead of time. This is a good requirement for program managers to impose on project managers. You can then review their top ten questions and answers prior to the presentation. As a result of this exercise, when someone in the audience asks a difficult question, the response is more confident. The audience will then naturally view the presenter as "in control" and knowledgeable.

4. **Know your graphics.** Unless you know that the decision maker or audience wants and expects a lot of charts and graphs, you should limit the amount of visual aids you provide. When I give a presentation, I never have more than ten charts. Now, I may have 267 backup charts queued up and ready to go, but unless I sense that my audience needs more charts, I stick to ten. While presenting, observe the body language and nonverbal clues of the decision maker. If he or she is on page eight and you are still talking about page two, that is a clue to speed up.

In fishing, there is a term known as "matching the hatch." That means you need to find out what the fish are eating now (usually whatever just hatched), and present them something that looks like that because they will readily eat it. The same applies for presentations. If my audience/decision makers are used to whiz-bang graphics with flying icons and fancy color handouts, that's what I give them. If they are used to plain vanilla, black-and-white presentations without using the projector, that's what I give them.

5. **Know "the look."** The same matching-the-hatch rule can apply for dress. If the environment is business casual, then "dressed-up" business casual may be acceptable if you are the presenter. If the audience is in suit and tie, then the presenter wearing a suit and tie is appropriate. If you can't

get an accurate assessment of the dress code, then remember that it is always better to be overdressed than underdressed. Jackets and ties are easily removed.

For any presentation, always arrive well ahead of time to take care of audio/visual technology issues. You look sophomoric if your presentation is scheduled to start at 10:00 a.m. and you are setting up or verifying your display unit works at 9:59 a.m. The five to ten minutes just prior to the presentation is usually invaluable from a relationship building point of view, as it allows you to mingle with your audience and talk with them in a casual way. Here you can likely head off issues or questions prior to the meeting in a more relaxed environment. You cannot leverage this time if you are tinkering with the technology. And if something proves not to work for some reason, always have a hard-copy backup handy.

During the presentation, be explicit about what you want the decision maker to do. Never assume that he or she will make the logical leap and do what is required or expected. You can even have a very specific bullet that says "I [or we or the XYZ program] need you to ―― by the 15th of next month." Then explain the ramification of what happens if ―― is not done. I had a training participant who had attended a number of my classes tell me that this one piece of advice had proven so valuable in his environment that it alone was worth his attendance in all of my classes.

Feedback Processes

It is very important that as program manager you engage in regular feedback activities with your project managers and stakeholders. Project managers should also be taught to give project team members feedback and the program manager should make sure this is taking place. Feedback provides the opportunity to improve your performance, and equally important is that when you request it, it then empowers you to give it back to the person you requested it from. This allows you to correct negative behavior or nonperformance issues in a graceful way. Feedback can help drive accountability.

Consistency is important here and feedback should be given to all, not just those who need an adjustment. Project milestones are feedback opportunities or they can simply be done on a monthly basis. Feedback can be a good tool for enabling project managers to improve performance in a matrix environment when project managers have little if any direct control over team members. Effective feedback is best obtained by not blaming, and it is critical to always be honest and future-focused, focusing on the behaviors you would like to see without criticizing past behaviors.

SCENARIO

I once heard a program manager emphatically accuse his organization of not doing what he specifically asked them to do. When I questioned him later about this, he said, "The organization didn't agree with what I had told them, so they exercised a pocket veto. They intentionally slowed down or worked other items to avoid my specific directions. When you see this sort of behavior, you need to realize that you probably haven't communicated why your request is important. Because if it really is important, then you ought to be able to make the case that it is and gain their buy-in to the action."

A very successful consultant told me that the reason he makes such a good living, that what helps him thrive at a high economic level, is listening—not just listening to understand, but listening specifically for the best way to communicate back to individuals what they need to hear in a way that makes them accept it and act upon it. He tailors the message so they won't discount it. He has found that people are open to ideas they agree with and are comfortable with, but that when it is out of this context he has to take extra time to facilitate discussion and craft his language so they will hear it within the context of their biases and frame of reference.

The program manager needs to take this into account in all communication processes.

KEYSTONES
Program Communication Processes

1. Program managers need to strategically choose program communication processes.
2. Communication processes are leadership processes not notifiership processes.
3. The program manager should define a structure, rules, and guidelines for all program meetings.
4. How well a program manager's project managers run and execute program meetings is a reflection of the program manager and the program itself.
5. Establishing a common title structure for e-mails increases productivity.
6. The team charter eliminates miscommunications that are rooted in false assumptions by establishing a framework of agreement for team interactions.
7. When it comes to global teams, you will never be able to read it all in a book or get it all in a training class.
8. Providing global team members a coach from the culture(s) they are working with is very effective.
9. The program manager has to look beyond the current task, deliverable, or project and build strong virtual teams that provide dividends for the life of the program.
10. How the program manager and program personnel make presentations is a reflection of the program's credibility and effectiveness.
11. Effective listening is not just listening to understand, but listening specifically for the best way to communicate back to individuals what they need to hear in a way that makes them accept it and act upon it.

Program Risk Management

Program managers must lead in an environment of uncertainty. Risk management processes serve to provide structure to handle this uncertainty. The uncertainty by itself is challenging enough, but if it is not handled with consistent methods, the uncertainty escalates. Therefore, the program manager needs to create a proactive and positive culture when it comes to risk management.

Risk Definition

Whenever the discussion of risk management occurs during one of my training events, invariably the attendees tell me there is a lot of confusion about what is a risk and what is not. They reveal that when they gather potential risks, they also end up gathering assumptions, issues, and questions. The challenge is then differentiating among (1) risks, (2) issues, (3) assumptions, and (4) questions. For consistency's sake and to ensure a successful program, you need to resolve this issue at the program level, and/or you need to work with the PMO to establish common definitions.

To provide some perspective, I will give my recommendation on how to define and categorize each of the four items just mentioned. However, the primary concern is that all of these risks, issues, assumptions, and questions are properly identified and characterized, and assigned to a single individual for management and/or resolution. Once that is done, what label something has isn't important, because it has been identified and assigned to someone for action. Therefore, consider the following definitions.

- *Risks* are events that are uncertain. Should they materialize, they will have either a positive or negative impact on the project or program.
- *Issues* are actionable items that require resolution or a decision. Once resolved, they may create or eliminate risks. Unresolved issues always create risks.
- *Assumptions* are items believed or presumed to be true as a basis for establishing plans or decision making. Sometimes an assumption may not be valid, and you need to establish response plans accordingly.
- *Questions* are items that need to be answered or addressed. Once questions are addressed, they may identify new risks, issues, or assumptions.

Based on the definitions above, the condition wherein the customer does not sign off on the requirements is an issue, and the program management leadership must resolve this issue. If it is left unresolved, the project manager must manage this issue like a risk.

In organizations that lack leadership, all issues must be managed as risks. Not only do unresolved issues create risks; they result from indecision and lead to a poor environment, breeding unsuccessful projects. Issue resolution is the program manager's domain—unresolved issues burden the project manager, and it is the program manager's responsibility to facilitate issue resolution in order to pave the way for success.

The Program Manager's Risk Environment

The program manager's risk environment is complex, because risks at the business level, program level, or project level can impact the program. That's why categorization of risks facilitates better risk identification activities. Additionally, the program manager must scrutinize which business- and program-level risks project mangers should address. It would be too burdensome and unnecessary for project managers to try to address all the risks that exist at each of these levels. Just as the program manager filters and decides what project managers need to address, the project manager also has to filter and decide what project-level risks are shown or escalated to the business level. Realize that the business level would be overwhelmed if its managers saw or even knew about every project-level risk.

So what are the various risks in each category? While not all-inclusive, the following are some common risks in each segment.

- Business-level risks are numerous and include increased government regulation, globalization and outsourcing, technology changes, changes in competition, changes in demand for the products and services provided, ownership changes occurring through merger or buyout, and rapid expansion or contraction of products and services provided.
- Program-level risks include budget cuts, reorganization, turnover of program personnel, stakeholder changes, cost overruns, and failed projects.

- Project-level risks include resources availability, implementation risks, technology risks, and changing stakeholders.

Informing Stakeholders

Risks in a program can be represented using an iceberg analogy. Certain risks are obvious and seen by everyone. Other risks are below the surface. The diligent program manager must know what's above the surface as well as what's below. The difficult program management question is: How much of what's below the surface needs to be communicated to stakeholders? Think of it this way: It is important for an airline pilot to communicate "turbulence ahead" to passengers, but passengers don't need to know that this is the airplane's first flight since the engines were replaced or that it's the pilot's first solo landing in a real jet.

Likewise, the program manager has to determine the degree of necessity of making stakeholders aware of all risks, and of any benefits of doing so. The other side of this coin is that stakeholders should never be surprised. When stakeholders know about the risk and the potential response and mitigation plans, psychologically the stakeholder is in a position of sharing the risk versus the risk being shouldered solely by the program or project manager. And when you do share a risk with a stakeholder, you also need to make him or her aware of how bad a situation can be or how ugly it can get.

Is one way right? It depends on your organizational culture and the nature of your stakeholders.

Risk Identification

The most important tool in the program manager's risk management arsenal is to be available and to listen. In fact, there are no substitutes for being available and for listening. Why? Because you cannot fix, avoid, or mitigate what you don't know. Being available and listening means paying attention to the process and the people, and constantly being on the lookout for changes and abnormalities within the program. It also means being able to put what you hear in the appropriate context of what it really means in the dynamic program environment. All program managers should know the process they use to bubble up problems and risks so that they can be heard and subsequently addressed. That's why the program manager must establish standardized processes for risk management. If there is a PMO in the organization, these processes may already exist. Even if they do exist, the program manager may have to tailor or adjust them to maximize value to the program.

As every program manager knows, it's a bad day at work when someone says, "Uh-oh. We didn't think about that." The program manager's job is to make sure that the project managers do a thorough and complete risk identification process. Some people like to use the word "unknowns" as an excuse for doing a poor job of risk identification. But if an unknown-risk event happens, that event should be so unknown and so out-of-the-box that no one would even ask whether it should have been identified. When project managers do a thorough and complete risk identification process, they will be unable to manage all of the risks because there will not be enough time or money to do so.

With all the risks identified, the program manager needs to come to agreement with each project manager as to where the line will be drawn on the project's risk lists. Risks above the line will be actively managed. Risks below the line will just be monitored and reassessed at the next appropriate time (usually the next milestone).

To say, "We didn't think about that," is poor program management. To say, "We identified it, assessed it, and made a conscious decision not to manage it based on available resources," is an acceptable answer. Bad things happen, and sometimes bad things happen to people who have done a good job.

Good risk decisions do not guarantee a good outcome. That's why the program manager must defend and shield project managers from persecution and scapegoating when they get an unfortunate outcome. Defending the project managers in this manner empowers them to continue making aggressive decisions.

TIP

I am continually amazed at the "free lunch" leaders that exist in some organizations. Free lunch leaders want something for nothing because of naivety or the willful intention to not be accountable. These leaders think that every risk should be managed, even when there are not enough resources. Resource limitations are real, and the leadership needs to decide on and/or buy into the trade-offs and resulting sacrifices.

Risk Assessment

Many risk management methods exist. Some methods are qualitative and some are quantitative. This chapter will focus on two methods that require the most program management leadership. One method is the Risk Response Matrix, and the other is the Five-by-Five Risk Matrix. The Risk Response Matrix requires program manager leadership because it develops responses across projects. The Five-by-Five Risk Matrix requires program manager intervention to establish and ensure that the qualitative criteria are applicable across the entire organization.

Risk Response Matrix

One effective tool for maximizing the value of limited resources is to assess major project risks across the program with a Risk Response Matrix. As illustrated in Figure 8.1, the matrix identifies risks in the

FIGURE 8.1 Risk Reponse Matrix

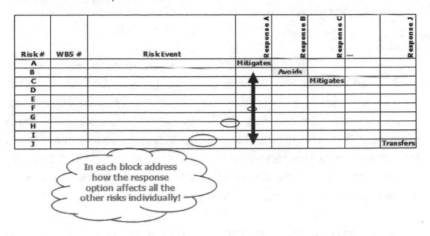

rows on the grid and the planned responses to the corresponding risk in the columns. You can easily manage such a matrix in Microsoft Excel. In each block of the matrix, you should indicate how the response option affects all the other risks individually.

You then evaluate each risk against the response for every other risk. The evaluation determines how the response impacts the risk. For example, does it mitigate the risk? Does it increase or decrease the impact? Does it increase or decrease the likelihood of the risks?

Within a program there are often undercurrents that are shared among projects. Thus, the response to a risk on one project can eliminate risk on other projects. Therefore, use of the Risk Response Matrix ensures that the best "program decision" is made when it comes to risk response. This may seem time-consuming and cumbersome to go through, but often it greatly simplifies the response planning required within the program. Remember, the Risk Response Matrix is an integration tool. What looks good, and what seems logical and straightforward in isolation, may be time-consuming and costly when viewed from the integrated perspective of the program manager or even the project manager of complex projects.

I was once involved with a Risk Response Matrix for an organization for which several hundred business-level risks existed. When the evaluation was complete, three primary responses were chosen that, after some logical and well-thought-out adaptation to the responses, addressed over 80 percent of all the risks and all of the major risks. Because of the Risk Response Matrix, the leadership was able to focus their efforts on these responses to the point that execution could be quickly implemented if a risk event materialized. Prior to the creation of the matrix, everyone had viewed their risks only from their own limited perspective.

A challenge to implementing the Risk Response Matrix is that it can become large and unwieldy. Prudent prioritization or limiting what risks will be included in the matrix is often necessary. For example, the program manager may create a Risk Response Matrix for the top five risks on the ten most important projects. Or a Risk Response Matrix could be created for all project risks of a program that have an impact in excess of $100,000, or whatever is the appropriate figure based on program scope. The point here is that you need to make sure the best-integrated responses to the most important program risks are chosen. Use of the tool also facilitates effective communication among project managers and serves to justify program stakeholders.

The Five-by-Five Risk Matrix

The use of qualitative risk tools has grown very popular, and the Five-by-Five Risk Matrix is one such tool that smart program managers deploy. Although project managers can apply qualitative risk analysis independently, the process of evaluating qualitative risks is a program requirement. Organizationally, if there is a PMO, the program manager must partner with the PMO and/or other program managers so that a qualitative risk management tool can be used effectively across the organization.

Qualitative risk analysis requires the development and refinement of ordinal scales to characterize the likelihood and impacts of risks. This is a fairly straightforward task when accomplished for a single project. But given the variety of projects across an organization, the development of the "one size fits all" qualitative tool is challenging. Once created, the tool also must get the buy-in of all organizational stakeholders with a formal sign-off.

Tailor the Risk Matrix

Fortunately, there are various ways to tackle the one-size-fits-all challenge. For example, I have one client who has two versions of his qualitative risk matrix—one for large projects and a simplified version (three-by-three matrix) for small projects. There is nothing magic about a Five-by-Five Risk Matrix. If four-by-four or three-by-three better suits your need, then use that. The key is consistency across the program and organization. Figure 8.2 shows a sample of a Five-by-Five Risk Matrix.

The Five-by-Five Risk Matrix characterizes probability and impact of certain risk factors. You obtain this characterization by multiplying a risk likelihood and risk impact score. You can show multiple risks on a single matrix, or you can maintain risks in tabular form by the score. The scores for likelihood and impact are assessed based on criteria established by the organization. Generic examples for this kind of criteria are shown in Table 8.1 and Table 8.2.

Using tailored tables of this type allows you to multiply the risk impact by the risk likelihood for the three elements of the triple constraint: time, cost, and scope. The scores for time, cost, and scope can be maintained or represented separately, or just use the highest of the three. Never add the three scores together, as it

FIGURE 8.2 Five-by-Five Risk Matrix

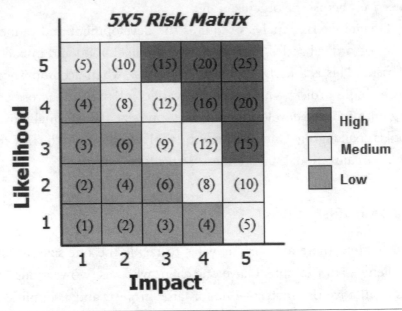

could mask a high-level risk if one element of the triple constraint had a high impact and the other two were very low. In addition to the elements of the triple constraint, you can develop other criteria, such as organizational reputation, to assess the impact of the risk on the organization's standing. This is the power of using qualitative techniques. You can easily tailor them to the circumstances that are most valuable to the organization. The key is to make it consistently applicable and agreed upon across the program and then the company if possible.

Assessing Probabilities. Assessing probabilities in the qualitative scheme can prove challenging. A convenient and effective way to estimate the probability is through a series of questions that split the probability of the event in half. The first question to ask the risk owner, the expert(s), or the team is: "Do you think the probability of this event is greater or less than 50 percent?" In most cases people can answer this with confidence.

TABLE 8.1 Impact Scale for Five-by-Five Risk Matrix

LEVEL	TIME	COST	SCOPE
5	Very High, >20 percent project budget slip	Very High, >20 percent of project budget	Very Difficult, outside of current experience base to maintain required scope
4	High, >10 percent project end date slip	High, >10 percent of project budget	Difficult, but within current experience base to maintain required scope
3	Moderate, >5 percent project end date slip or >20 percent milestone slip	Moderate, >5 percent of project budget or 20 percent of task budget	Moderate difficulty within current experience base to maintain required scope
2	Low, >10 percent milestone slip and <5 percent project end date slip	Low, >10 percent of task budget and <5 percent of project budget	Standard processes can resolve it to maintain required scope
1	Very Low, <10 percent milestone slip, without project end date slip	Very Low, <10 percent of task budget and <5 percent of project budget	Easily resolved to maintain required scope

TABLE 8.2 Likelihood Scale for Five-by-Five Risk Matrix

LEVEL	LIKELIHOOD	PROBABILITY
5	Very High	85% to 100%
4	High	65% to 84%
3	Moderate	35% to 64%
2	Low	15% to 34%
1	Very Low	0% to 14%

If they answered "less than 50 percent," then the next question to ask is: "Do you think the probability is between 25 and 50 percent or less than 25 percent?" Again, in most cases people can answer this with confidence.

If they answered "less than 25 percent" then the next question to ask is: "Do you think the probability is between 12½ and 25 percent or less than 12½ percent?" Sometimes people can answer this question with confidence. Sometimes they can't.

The intent of these questions is to narrow down the percent range until you reach a level where people are indifferent between the choices. Once you reach this level, the conservative approach for evaluation is to accept the highest level of risk at their indifference level as to the probability of risk. For example, if someone thought the risk was between 0 and 25 percent, but could not discriminate whether it was less than 12½ or between 12½ and 25 percent, you would use 25 percent for the likelihood scale in the qualitative risk matrix.

Establish Common Definitions. Some organizations use words without sufficient definition behind them, and the interpretation by different personnel can often lead to inconsistent results. For example, if they use descriptors like "very low," "low," "medium," "high," and "very high," my interpretation of "high" and someone else's interpretation of "high" may not be the same thing.

Once likelihood and impacts are set, you can plot the risks on the matrix. Since the matrix scoring is obtained by multiplying the likelihood and the impact, the resulting scores from all assessed risks can be prioritized based on their scores.

Using the matrix provides a consistent way to evaluate risks across the organization. Once the structure is complete, escalation of important risks occurs through the process. In some programs the program manager is briefed weekly on the status of all red (very high) risk items. This serves to "bubble up" the risks the program manager needs to be cognizant of.

In the Five-by-Five Risk Matrix, items that have an impact of 5 and a likelihood of 1 or 2 are normally designated yellow or medium risk. However, these are and should be red in any organization.

Even if something has a very low likelihood, if the impact can be devastating to the program, the risk should be aggressively managed. Employing risk management tools can be an effective way to manage risks across an organization, but as with any tool, keen judgment is always vital.

Question Data. Quantitative methods for risk management are based on data. Their use for the majority of projects is straightforward, providing you have valid data or the data is used and presented in the range of its accuracy. When it comes to data, the program manager needs to ask questions to ensure its validity. I learned the hard way not to be surprised when, after you have questioned the source of some data, you find that the data is not credible. Additionally, people have a dangerous tendency to assume they know what is between two data points, and that what is between those two points is linear. Whenever you observe program personnel making assumptions about what lies between two data points or circumstances, question them thoroughly on those assumptions.

Establish Adequate Reserve

One of the program manager's responsibilities is to establish adequate amounts of reserve to handle risks. How the amount of reserve is established may vary, from using expected value (probability of occurrence times cost impact) to just taking a percentage of the overall program budget for projects. In many organizations, 10 to 20 percent is typically held back for reserve. Whatever percentage you use, make sure it's established based on the organization's history of project overruns and by factoring in the expected value of the risk events for the project. The program manager needs to be cognizant of the biggest risks in a program, because in

the real world of program and project management we get outcomes, not averages. The amount of reserve determined should
factor in what would be done if for some unfortunate reason a few
major risks materialized.

It is then up to the program manager to "sell" the reserve amount
in the budget process to ensure allocation to the program. Thus,
when choosing and developing risk management tools, give consideration to how these tools can be used to bolster the credibility
of the rationale used to justify the reserve amount. This is another
reason for having adequate data on the program's previous performance and project implementation success rate.

Once a reserve amount has been established for the program,
the program manager then must decide who will have access to
this information. In some organizations it is public knowledge. In
others it is a closely guarded secret. I believe that the more people
there are who know about the reserve amount, the greater is the
likelihood that some will try to use it. Because of this philosophy,
some organizations establish no reserve. However, when program
reserves are inadequate or nonexistent, the program manager
must be prepared to "rob" other projects within the program if
necessary. Nothing comes for free. And in "no reserve" environments some program managers will create a place-holder project
(a low-priority project) that will be used to hide reserve. Most
experienced program or project managers that are not allowed
reserves or who have had their budget indiscriminately reduced
become very adept at building clandestine reserves into their project or program.

Keep Project Managers Focused on Risks

As a program manager, you need to ensure that project managers
are actively engaged in managing risks. Therefore, during meetings

with project managers, always ask about each project manager's top-ten risk list. You can also conspicuously post the top-ten list for each project in your office or in the conference room. This serves as a visual reminder to everyone that all the risks are important and worthy of attention.

Program managers should also sign off on the risk management plan, even for small projects whose plan may be very informal. Additionally, monthly or quarterly risk reviews with each project manager can give program managers an in-depth look at project risks. Remember, the program manager has to stay engaged with project risks so that project managers stay engaged. Preparation for these reviews is usually minimal so long as everyone is keeping up with the risks like they are supposed to.

TIP

A project manager in a recent risk management class asked, "If we do a good job on the risk management plan in the beginning of the project, then do we really need to review it again?" My response was that if the job on the risk management plan was that good, then the review should be quick and painless. I further stated that when the organization knows additional reviews will take place, people take the time to do a good job in the first place.

Risk Attitudes

Program managers need to establish a consistent method for evaluating and responding to risk across the enterprise. One obstacle to consistency in managing risk is that people naturally have different attitudes toward risks, and these attitudes vary according to the circumstance. The three primary characteristics that describe risk attitudes are "risk seeking," "risk neutral," and "risk averse." You exhibit a risk-seeking attitude when you are willing to pay a premium or penalty to accept a risk; a risk neutral one when your decisions are based solely on expected monetary value; and a risk averse one when you are willing to pay a premium or penalty to avoid risk.

The average person is usually risk averse. For example, if you purchase any kind of insurance protection over and above what the law requires, you are exhibiting risk averse behavior. The program manager has to recognize that successful organizations often perform best when they are aggressive and risk seeking, even though project managers may naturally be risk averse.

This is further complicated because our risk attitude is usually a function of wealth. For example, psychologists often argue that the lottery is a tax on the poor. Because of their low state of wealth, the poor buy disproportionately more lottery tickets than do members of other economic classes. They have "nothing to lose" in comparison with the prize. If you doubt this, consider the behavior of many potential lottery ticket buyers. When there is a huge jackpot of over $75 million or $100 million, people who don't normally purchase lottery tickets buy some. The reason is that people who are not considered "poor" by society's standards suddenly consider themselves poor in comparison with the $75 million prize. That's when they become risk seeking.

While there are never absolutes when dealing with human behavior and attitudes, in general people are more risk seeking in a poor state and more risk averse in a wealthy state. You frequently observe risk averse behavior in sport's team coaches who have a large lead in a game, as this puts them in a high-wealth state. They got the large lead by being aggressive, but the large lead causes them to change tactics to a more conservative "lead protection" strategy. This risk averse lead-protection strategy often works to their detriment, and they either barely win the game or lose the game because their risk attitude caused them to change their previously successful strategy that created the lead in the first place.

Why is this important to the program manager who is trying to manage risk consistently? It is because a project manager's risk attitude can be a function of his or her perceived "state of wealth" of the project. That is, the project manager of a "wealthy" project that is on schedule, with adequate budget and no issues, may be reluctant to make aggressive or risky decisions because of an underlying "risk averse" attitude ("Let's not rock the boat now"). Conversely, a project manager of a project that is behind schedule and over budget may be overly aggressive because of having an underlying "risk seeking" attitude due to a perceived low-wealth state ("There is nothing to lose; we are already late and over budget").

Realize that neither decision in the previous two examples is wrong. The point is that in general, project managers on stable projects may miss or purposefully forgo opportunities because they are not risk seeking enough. Likewise, project managers on projects in desperate circumstances may employ too many "desperate" risk-seeking measures (reducing testing requirements) due to their underlying risk attitude. The program manager must be aware of the strong biases of risk attitudes on decisions and take them into account.

When dealing with projects that are very stable and performing well, you need to ask the project manager, "If we had to deliver this project 25 percent sooner (or 25 percent cheaper), what would be the top three recommendations you would make to achieve this?" This forces the "wealthy state" risk averse project manager to think like a risk-seeking project manager and facilitate the risk/reward trade-off analysis. When addressing project managers of projects that are behind schedule and/or over budget, the question should be, "If none of the schedule and/or cost pressure were in this project right now, what are the conservative decisions we would take to ensure a quality deliverable?" This forces the "poor state of wealth" risk-seeking project manager to think like a risk averse project manager and ensures the current plans of action to be put into proper context. Remember, we want the best decision for the circumstances regardless of the underlying risk attitude.

Be Success Oriented

A major part of how an organization performs risk management is the attitude the leader takes with regard to risk. That means the leader has to be positive when dealing with risk so that the positive attitude migrates to the team. The leader always sets the tone, especially in the face of adversity or high-risk situations. Risk and adversity are part of the program manager's daily diet. That's why the program manager must focus on the positive, have a vision of success, and communicate that vision. This also involves keeping stakeholders up-to-speed and reassuring them during risky periods. Good commercial airline pilots are very adept at doing this with passengers. If there is turbulence ahead, they advise the passengers over the intercom. If there are unusual circumstances, they advise passengers how the circumstances will be handled.

The program manager has a similar role. He or she must keep the program passengers reassured and tell them when to "fasten their seat belts." The program manager must focus the project managers on what they can control or influence. Anything that is beyond that may or may not be addressed with a response plan. In fact, a lot of things that exist at the project level that people spend time worrying about should be ignored. Even worse, often one or two people search for any reason to worry, create worry in others, or look for an excuse to slow down or stop working. The program manager must make sure project managers recognize their job and their teams' job is to finish regardless of the circumstances flying around them.

For example, I am aware of two major telecommunications companies who were going to merge. For the better part of a year the focus was on the merger to the degree that projects were stalled or put on hold. In the end, the merger didn't happen, and a significant amount of productivity was lost. That's why program managers have to keep project managers focused on finishing, regardless of the dynamic circumstances outside of the program or project environment.

In another company I knew a project manager who would say, "That is too big a problem to be a problem." What he meant by this statement was that there were certain risks that, if they materialized, could not have been prevented by mitigation plans at his level, because the project would now be meaningless in light of the new circumstances. So he would follow up the "That is too big a problem to be a problem" statement with: "Our job is to continue to be aggressive and finish this project and let the large-scale things beyond our job description and control work themselves out."

SCENARIO

Finally, consider this: The probability for loss of a space shuttle during a mission is sometimes debated, but most agree that it is around 1 in 100, whether you consider historical data or sophisticated failure mode analysis. One out of 100 is high risk for an impact of this magnitude. To put this in perspective, the United States Federal Aviation Administration (FAA) manages around 50,000 flights per day. So if the space shuttle potential failure statistic applied to the FAA, the 1 in 100 failure rate would equate with 500 plane crashes every day (if we didn't run out of planes and people were still willing to fly).

Astronauts know the risk is high. NASA leadership knows the risk is high. Even so, they cannot and do not focus on the negative. They have to focus on doing what they know how to do and doing it very well and then they will be successful on launch day.

They can't afford to dwell on the significant probability of failure, even when that probability is real. How would you feel if your doctor advised you to have a surgical procedure and every time you saw him he reminded you of the failure rate of the procedure? If you are focusing on failure, it will find you. The program manager's responsibility is to be success oriented and migrate that success orientation throughout the program. That means managing risks without being disheartened by risk so that he or she can predispose the team to success. The program manager's role is to create an environment that fosters project success. And how the program manager addresses risk management is a vital part of the successful project environment.

Program Risk Management

1. The primary concern is that all risks, issues, assumptions, and questions are identified, properly characterized, and assigned to a single individual for management and/or resolution.
2. The program manager has to determine the necessity or benefit of risks in order to determine which risks to make stakeholders aware of.
3. The most important tool in the program manager's risk management arsenal is to be available and to listen.
4. Good risk decisions do not guarantee a good outcome. The program manager must defend and shield project managers from persecution and scapegoating when they get an unfortunate outcome.
5. Use of the Risk Response Matrix ensures that the best "program decision" is made when it comes to risk response.
6. The power of using qualitative techniques is that they can be easily tailored to the circumstances that are most valuable to the organization.
7. The level of program and project reserve should be based on the organization's history of project overruns and by factoring in the expected value of the risk events for the project.
8. Quarterly risk reviews with each project manager can give program managers an in-depth look at project risks.
9. People naturally have different attitudes toward risks, and these attitudes vary according to the circumstance and will impact their response to risks. The program manager must ensure the best decision for the circumstances regardless of the underlying risk attitude.
10. The leader has to be positive when dealing with risk so that the positive attitude migrates to the team.

Portfolio Management Essentials

More has probably been written about project portfolio management in the last decade than in all other decades combined. As the project management profession matures, the number of software tools that claim to control and maximize the value of the organization's portfolio of projects increases dramatically. While there is nothing wrong with these tools, my observations and experience lead me to believe that many organizations are not ready for a sophisticated portfolio management tool. Why? It is because a lot of organizations haven't yet mastered the basics of portfolio management. Before any tool is purchased and rolled out, the basics must be in place.

A portfolio can include multiple programs, and/or the projects within a single program can be a portfolio. A portfolio is just a logical grouping of projects under a common leadership structure.

Strategic Management of Portfolio Resources

Buying a fancy tool is no substitute for discipline. Unfortunately, some program managers want tools to tell them what to do. In reality, no tool should tell a program manager what to do. Tools are just inputs to the decision maker's judgment process. Any tool should ensure thoroughness and structure the information in a way that allows the decision maker to make a decision. This includes helping the decision maker know what information is firm, what information is fuzzy, how the information was processed, what information was excluded, and what the tool may recommend. The decision maker then must assess all the input before factoring in his or her experience or intuition and making the actual decision.

TIP

I have helped several organizations in both the public and private sectors establish value structures, managing portfolios that have exceeded $1 billion as well as very small portfolios. During the process, I typically encounter two types of decision makers: One type is scared to death that the tool will dictate what to do without his or her judgment, and the other is scared to death the tool won't dictate to him or her exactly what to do. Remember, tools are there to provide structure and an accurate representation of all the factors relevant to the decision, not to dictate to the decision maker or to relieve him or her of responsibility. Even though a tool may provide a recommended list of projects, the judgment of the decision maker should prevail.

Know Your Resource Availability

All successful portfolios follow two important guidelines. First is to regulate capacity utilization and second is to prioritize the portfolio.

Regulate Capacity Utilization

In order to produce a valid strategy, you must know exactly what your resources are. Some organizations go through all of the trouble of identifying and selecting projects, establishing a "supposed" portfolio, but in the end all they really have are ten gallons' worth of projects and only a five-gallon bucket. So they exceed the organization's capacity. Consider Figure 9.1, which shows a typical relationship (from the book *Creating an Environment for Successful Projects* by Robert J. Graham and Randall L. Englund).

FIGURE 9.1 Multiple Project Overload

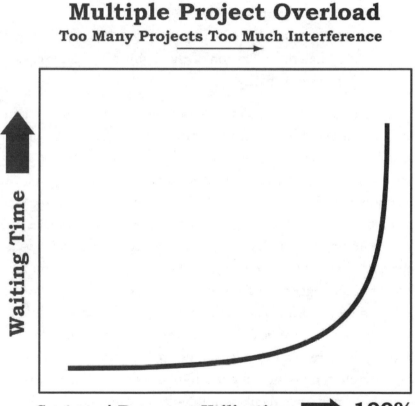

Multiple Project Overload
Too Many Projects Too Much Interference

This relationship is basically true for any system! Exceeding 90% capacity for projects in an organization causes serious inefficiencies

Source: Robert J. Graham and Randall L. Englund, *Creating an Environment for Succesful Projects.* Jossey Bass, 1997.

The figure shows that as system utilization increases, interference in the system also increases. The increase becomes rapid as system utilization approaches 100 percent. This is basically true for any system! Exceeding 90 percent capacity for projects in an organization causes serious inefficiencies. If this is not intuitive to you, consider the following examples.

- Your computer. As your CPU utilization, your computer memory, or your disk drive start to exceed 90 percent of capacity, the system slows dramatically because of interference in the system.
- A highway system. Traffic jams and slowdowns will always occur when the utilization of the highway system exceeds 90 percent of capacity.

Organizations that regulate input to ensure that capacity is controlled and that the system utilization rarely exceeds 90 percent actually accomplish more over a year's timeframe than organizations that don't regulate input. Additionally, when the system is operating at high utilization, small abnormalities (for example, one project's design review being delayed by two weeks, just like one person cutting off another on a highway), can cause major backups and slowdowns. Even worse, the slowdown may continue long after the trigger event is over, often to the degree that the trigger cannot be identified or remembered.

Organizations that deal with physical deliverables typically do a better job at regulating capacity utilization, because exceeding capacity often has visual physical indicators and limits that show themselves and force regulation. Regulating capacity utilization is much more difficult for information technology organizations, where there are no "physical limits" to restrict the appetite of a management structure that is always putting one more project on the table. Regardless, exceeding the resource requirements of an organization is the root cause for many organizational deficiencies.

Characteristics of an organization with a high degree of interference include frequent changes in priorities and constant fire fighting. Interestingly, sometimes job satisfaction can be high in these kinds of environments, because of the rush that results when a problem is fixed. That rush can be so addictive that people may be dissatisfied when there is not a fire to fight or an emergency to respond to. Thus, the organization has to guard against creating and/or attracting personnel who simply like to fight fires and deal with short-term tasks.

Often, the very capable planning type of individual may not stay in such an environment long or may become apathetic. Over longer periods of time the organization will attract and retain the kinds of personnel that the environment rewards. What gets rewarded gets repeated. Therefore, the program manager has to ensure that the program operates at a capacity that maximizes output over the long term. This means the input has to be regulated, because there will always be more work than the organization can accomplish.

When I present the relationship of system utilization and interference, the audience identifies with and agrees with the premise of not exceeding organizational capacity. But invariably, someone asks me the complex question: "How do you measure organizational capacity?" This is a difficult question to answer, especially for IT organizations, and I do not have a precise answer for it. However, you can estimate projects and estimate resource requirements against resource allocations. Granted, these are only estimates and they often assume the existence of a lot of intangibles. But if the program manager is in touch with the organization and has a feel for what is transpiring at the working level, he or she will know if the organization's capacity has been exceeded. Unstable calendars, lots of resource conflicts, frequent emergency situations, and delayed projects are all symptomatic of an organization that has exceeded capacity. Once again, you may have tools at your disposal, but sound judgment in the use of those tools will allow for good decisions.

Prioritize the Portfolio

The second guideline to portfolio success is to prioritize everything in the portfolio. I have heard some leaders make the statement that "everything is top priority." However, there is no such thing as "everything is top priority." Simple logic proves that if everything is top priority, then everything is of equal priority. If everything is of equal priority, then the statement "everything is top priority" also means "everything is bottom priority." A sure sign of a lack of leadership is the statement "everything is top priority."

Everything is top priority basically says: "We leaders can't decide, so you decide" and "We leaders don't want to be accountable for what is not completed, but we want to hold you accountable for everything." It is easy to say that everything is a top priority, but the leader's role is to put things in priority order.

If the leader declares that everything is a top priority, what is the likelihood that 10, 15, or 100 personnel within a program are all working on the same top-priority items? Little or none! Lack of a leader-established priority order contributes to an ineffective program. And lack of priority order combined with working an organization beyond its capacity creates an organization characterized by dementia—a disoriented organization that is unable to consistently cognitively function.

In the absence of a priority list, program personnel will tend to work on what they like to do first, and then on tasks that are short and easy. The only thing that bumps these in the prioritization process is when someone is yelling for something. In fact, organizations that say "everything is top priority" typically end up playing the "yelling game," where everyone in need yells, whines, or plays politics to get their task done. Thus, the best yellers, whiners, or politicians often get their work accomplished regardless of its real importance to the organization.

Another pitfall here is a form of "hero worship." Yellers who want something done tend to go back to the person who last bailed them out. Sometimes they go directly to that person, violating the chain of command or program structure. The resource wants to be appreciated by the "hero," so they do "favors" for the yeller. Yelling is prevented but an abusive relationship is spawned. The yeller now knows that he can quietly call up Sally Sue and get what he wants. This creates absolute havoc. Therefore, even if your organization cannot regulate work so that you don't exceed 90 percent of capacity, you should at the very least establish and maintain a published prioritized list of projects (including problem fixes and opportunities).

The Basics of Portfolio Management

There are three commonsense categories of past, present, and future when dealing with the basics of portfolio management: (1) assessing where your program has been, (2) understanding where your program is today, and (3) driving where your program is going.

Assessing Where Your Program Has Been

Spanish philosopher George Santayana said, "Those who cannot learn from history are doomed to repeat it." His words can apply to program management. Unfortunately, many organizations do not look back at the preceding year with enough thoroughness. That is why a good program manager should look back at the preceding year and document the following:

1. What were the business's goals and targets for the year?
2. What was the variance of actual results compared with those goals?
3. What was the root cause of each variance?

202 THE HANDBOOK OF PROGRAM MANAGEMENT

This is important information to have. First, it documents that there were/are/should have been definitive goals and targets. You cannot calculate variances against nondefinitive targets. Second, establishing a root cause for the reason the goal was not met or exceeded can sometimes tell us how good we are at setting goals. No matter how good the execution, if the goals are not set properly then the results will not be satisfactory.

One school of thought says that goals should be "stretch goals," which are beyond the organization's current reach. There is nothing wrong with such thinking, but there is the danger that if the stretch goal is set too high, the organization could deem it unreachable. Once that happens, everyone will stop striving toward it . . . or toward anything else, for that matter. People will stretch for the achievable, but they won't move a muscle for the unachievable.

To plan for the future you need to analyze further what has been done in the previous year:

1. What projects were in the works when the previous year started?
2. Were any new projects born or created during the year?
3. What projects were completed during the year?
4. Were any projects terminated during the year?

To accurately characterize the workload for the year, you also need to obtain the following information:

- What organizational problems, opportunities, or challenges existed or were first identified during the year?
- Which of these were solved, resolved, or otherwise acted upon during the year?

A proper analysis of this information shows how well the organization is maturing. Are more problems being solved than are being created? Are any problems being solved? Do the same organizational problems exist year after year?

Most organizations do not have the resources to work through every project, fix every problem, and leverage every opportunity. So the program manager needs to assess how well the team did at working through the right projects, fixing the right problems, and leveraging the right opportunities while meeting goals and targets.

TIP

An assessment does not have to be the kind you pay a consultant for. Simply give yourself a grade on a scale of 1 to 10 for each question, and document the top three things that have room for improvement. Realistically examining past performance provides you with valuable information to help you make credible decisions.

Unfortunately, because of the prevalent "the customer is always right" mentality, many customers propose projects without full or even marginal understanding of what they are trying to accomplish or what they are changing. This problem is compounded when the organization does *not* measure the success of the project after delivery. In fact, too many organizations measure project success by evaluating it on only the triple constraints of time, cost, and scope for the implementation. They judge the project manager but not the customer. You also need to evaluate project success based on whether the project delivered the business value it promised. And before that value can be accurately assessed, the business unit requesting the project must provide measurable requirements logically tied to the project's purpose and measurable goals.

Some companies routinely implement projects with no real measure of whether the projects truly added value to the organization. Where this is allowed, customers often run amok with project requests. Now, if it is an external customer with huge resources to spend, thus creating revenue for your program, it may be to your short-term advantage to implement projects of questionable value; however, in the long term there is no substitute for providing value.

A lack of customer accountability for the success of their projects breeds a culture where the customers cry "give, give, give" and are never satisfied. Over time, the customers never improve at project selection, because they have never objectively measured the success of their previous selections. Furthermore, this creates an environment where progress is often evaluated by how many projects are being proposed within a particular business segment, because change—any change—is considered progress. In reality, the true measure of progress is bottom-line results. Measuring the effectiveness of projects after delivery causes customers and stakeholders to carefully consider projects before proposing them. It creates an "accountability" culture in which people submit high-value projects.

Understanding Where Your Program Is Today

Understanding where the program is today will involve some of the same fundamental questions we just addressed for the prior year, except now you'll address them in the context of this year. The questions are:

1. What are the business goals and targets for the current year?
   a. Are the goals realistic?
   b. What do you assess as the likelihood you will achieve each of the goals?

The question regarding business goals and targets is necessary, because all organizations do not have documented targets and goals. Some organizations that have them often do not maintain them, or the goals have existed for years or since the "founder" set them.

Business goals and targets should create tangible objectives that meet the SMART test. SMART stands for Specific, Measurable,

Agreed upon, Realistic, and Time constrained. Having a business goal of being the "leading provider of Gobbledygook widgets and services" is meaningless without qualification as to what that means. After all, what does "leading provider" mean? How do you know when you've attained that status, specifically? When should that goal become reality? Is it even possible?

Often, the program manager may be responsible for attaining such a vague goal. It is then up to him or her to characterize what "leading provider" means and to obtain buy-in on the characterization from stakeholders. Depending upon where the organization currently is and the resources it has available, there may be a time-phased plan with annual targets for the next five years. Organizations sometimes set goals that are unachievable and it is the program manager's responsibility to work with stakeholders to establish achievable goals.

    2. What projects . . .
        a. Are currently in work and part of the portfolio?
            (1) Were in the works when the previous year started?
            (2) Were born or created during this year?
        b. Were completed already this year?
        c. Have been terminated during this year?
        d. Are in danger of being terminated this year?

The questions about project status are important in order to define what projects the organization actually has in work.

SCENARIO

For example, I once spoke with an organizational leader at a government agency who was moved to another part of the agency. He was surprised to learn that there was a lack of solid business goals and targets in this new (to him) part of the agency, and this lack of goals created program managers who were not guided properly. The result was that some of the program managers had done nothing new for years, while others were all over the map spending resources and implementing projects that were way out of the scope of the organizational mission.

When portfolio planning, you need a catalog of all projects in work within the organization. Certainly the program manager must have this for his or her program, but the program manager also needs to be concerned about projects in work outside of the program in shared-resource environments. Rogue projects outside of the program manager's control could be consuming resources that slow the work of projects within the program manager's control.

The question about projects being terminated is a necessary one. Examine the project failures and overruns your organization has had in the past few years. Assess whether the termination of the project at an earlier timeframe would have saved resources. Remember the concept of "sunk costs." People tend to want to recover lost or spent funds and adopt the false and dangerous logic of "we have already invested or spent this much, so we might as well see it through to the end." In reality, all that matters is the business case on the cost and revenues from this point forward. How much has already been spent or gone down the drain is immaterial.

Organizations sometimes have a problem acknowledging failure. But the sooner you acknowledge failure, the greater will be the cost savings.

SCENARIO

For instance, a major telecommunications company rolled out a new service on which they spent triple-digit millions before it was terminated because it didn't work as advertised. Many technical personnel and employees knew the service would not work well over a year before it was finally terminated. So why did the project continue? It did so because when a few employees brought their findings to the attention of the leadership early in the program, it proved to be a career-limiting move. After witnessing what happened to their peers, other employees just kept quiet until the program imploded.

Implosion is what you want to avoid. You can avoid implosion by putting poorly performing programs and projects up for termination review and terminating bad programs and projects quickly. Kill what's ugly while it is young. Additionally, during the portfolio-planning cycle, every project that is in work should be assessed. The question that should be specifically asked is: "What are the advantages of terminating this project now?" Carry-over from one fiscal year to another should not be automatic.

- What organizational problems or challenges do you currently have? What organizational problems were identified this year? The question about organizational problems is important because problems and challenges birth projects to fix them. Even if it is not a full-blown project that fixes a problem, the problem fix usually consumes resources. Additionally, every problem has an associated cost, including slower workflow, additional waste, and/or increased overhead.

- What opportunities do you currently have? What new opportunities were identified this year? The question about opportunities is important because opportunities can birth new projects. Also, there may be significant opportunities if the organization is looking for them. The program manager needs to establish a mind-set of people always looking for opportunity. Asking the question about opportunities and then aggressively following through on potential opportunities demonstrates that the program manager and the organization value opportunities.

- What are the greatest risks the program is now facing? You need to identify the major risks to the program for the current performance period. Resources may have to be set aside to account for these risks, and that impacts the portfolio.

- Are the targets, goals, projects, problems, opportunities, and risks in priority order? The leadership should establish what is most important. As mentioned earlier, putting the work in priority order is one of two keys to successful portfolio management.

Driving Where Your Program Is Going

A complete understanding of where you have been and an understanding of where your program is currently, combined with the requirements not to exceed workforce capacity and to provide prioritized leadership, becomes the basis of establishing a valid and viable portfolio that documents where the program is going.

Unfortunately, a lot of organizations buy fancy and sophisticated portfolio management tools without assessing where your program has been or understanding where your program is. The result can be time and money wasted on a tool that doesn't work or that selects the wrong projects.

When considering new projects for the portfolio, you need to answer three essential questions. These questions should usually be answered before a business case is developed, and they should be answered at least to a reasonable level of confidence before resources are spent, creating a full-fledged business case. The three questions are:

- Why do this at all?
- Why do it this way?
- Why do it now?

These questions can be attributed to the book *Principles of Engineering Economy* by Eugene L. Grant, et al. I first came across them over twenty-five years ago and they have served me well. These questions should have rock-solid answers. Answering them ensures that you engage in some forethought before spending resources to prepare a project for approval. Some organizations just create projects on "whims" of their stakeholders with little credible justification for the project.

I often encounter companies that are overworked, while at the same time implementing projects of questionable or no real value to their customers. These projects are the ones that add or modify business processes that are not understood, either by the customer or the organization. As a result, the project's requirements are often poorly defined. No customer or stakeholder should be allowed to change or fix anything that he or she doesn't understand.

The program manager has to ensure that project managers help the customer as required so that there is understanding. Yes, there are auditable, traceable criteria for understanding, and those are described below.

Before implementing any project that creates or changes a business process, be sure you address the following questions:

1. Does the customer understand the process being created or changed by the proposed project? Understanding means the process has been mapped to identify bottlenecks, failure-risk points, and other elements whose improvement can be measured. If the process is not mapped, it is not understood. . . . Period. If they understand it, mapping is easy.

   Having been involved in my share of process mapping and analysis, I can assure you that the results can be surprising. What everyone considers to be "the Problem" prior to the process mapping may not be the actual problem, but rather a symptom of "the Real Problem"—the root cause of the symptom (often of several symptoms). Treating symptoms is dangerous business, because it means the problem hasn't gone away; the root cause will continue to grow and ultimately create more symptoms that need to be cured.

2. Have the key components/measures of the process being identified? Every process has a few key components or drivers. A simple Pareto analysis should identify these. If metrics for these key process components do not yet exist, establish them now.

3. Has the natural process variation for the overall process and its key components/measures been calculated? Every component has natural process variation associated with it. Natural process variation tells you the typical range of the component/measure. Natural process variation is calculated based on historical data and is not estimated unless it is a brand-new process.

4. How much is the project estimated to improve the process and its key components? Since the natural process variation is known, the customer should be able to establish the impact (business goals) of the changes the project will provide on the component/metric.

If the preceding four questions can be answered with credibility, then you have a worthy project. If not, the project should be removed from consideration until there is understanding. This may sound harsh or unrealistic to some. However, I cannot overemphasize how counterproductive it is to fix or change what is not understood. While we may know we have a problem to fix, common sense demands that we understand the problem we are fixing. We must be able to specify the current problem's location in the process and set measurable goals for the outcome of the correction.

Business Cases

The business case for new projects and initiatives is a necessary step to ensure that they are worthy of consideration before implementation. Like any process, the business case can be structured with varying degrees of rigor depending upon dollar value, risk, or criticality to the organization. Creation of business cases shouldn't overwhelm the organization, and the program manager needs to be on guard to make sure the process of business case development does not become overly bureaucratic. Business cases should ensure that a thorough analysis of the potential opportunity has been performed. Should the initial case prove worthy of further pursuit, the program manager or portfolio management team now has the opportunity to identify areas that require additional details or further information. You can consider many factors in a business case, but the program manager has to regulate this process so that it remains efficient.

In the field of decision sciences there is a term known as "requisite," which basically means you have the information necessary for the decision. Requisite does not include unnecessary or ancillary information. With business cases, the danger for any tool or template is the inclusion of information that is not required for the decision. Not only do people waste time gathering the unnecessary information, but they also waste time sorting and analyzing the information. The program manager should require only requisite information in the business case.

It's still a good idea to have a place in a business case model that allows a person the opportunity to express why his or her "instincts" say the initiative will be a success. Many people overlook the value of instinct because it is not quantifiable and not part of what is considered "modern" management practices. However, instinct is often more valuable today, because change is occurring so rapidly that predicting success by quantifiable means is more and more problematic.

Business cases typically include:

- An overview of the project, including all the relevant background information. (Once approved this information is the basis for completing quadrant 1 on the project status sheet outlined in Chapter 5.)
- The project objectives, including how they relate to the program and/or business objectives.
- The scope of the project. At the business case level a good scope description should also include what is out of scope

and any other major assumptions relating to the project. Significant risks may also be included.

- The project execution strategy with key milestones and anticipated impacts (positive or negative) to other projects or ongoing operations.
- A financial breakdown including anticipated cash/resource flow requirements and financial metrics like Return on Investment (ROI) or Net Present Value (NPV). This financial breakdown should also include maintenance and disposal costs of the project deliverables.

Financial Measures

Return on Investment (ROI) is probably the most popular business case measure for assessing projects and initiatives. However, it is fraught with pitfalls and is the most overrated project selection method. I am using ROI here to represent a variety of financial measures that can be determined by financial analysis. Regardless of the final measure, whether it is Net Present Value (NPV), Internal Rate of Return (IRR), Economic Value Added (EVA), or ROI, the basis of the calculations is the same. You're looking for a forecast of revenue and costs.

I am certainly neither the first nor the only one to make disparaging remarks about financial measures. In the landmark book *Winning at New Products: Accelerating Ideas from Idea to Launch*, Robert G. Cooper, who is credited for development of the "stage gate" process, also passes judgment on financial measures like ROI as a project selection tool. When discussing project selection methods, this is what he had to say about financial measures for project selection:

> *These methods are extremely popular project selection approaches. But don't be fooled: The businesses with the poorest performing*

portfolios rely almost exclusively on financial selection approaches, according to our research.

ROI is computed using a forecast of costs and a forecast of revenue or cost savings. Thus, ROI is dependent upon the accuracy of the forecasts for the costs and revenue projections. The question that the program manager needs to ask is: "How accurate are, and what degree of confidence do you have in, these forecast estimates?" This question should be followed by a review of all the ROI estimates for the past three to five years to assess the demonstrated history of individual and organizational forecasting ability.

If the organization has a history of accurate costs and revenue forecasting, then have confidence in the ROI numbers. However, if the history of the organization's cost and revenue numbers is poor, the program manager should discount or ignore the ROI calculations. Still, have the organization calculate the ROI so you can judge their forecasting ability in the future, but you should not include ROI as a determining factor in your analysis to identify the best projects and initiatives.

As always, judgment is a determining factor, and if there is overwhelming and compelling evidence leading you to consider ROI, despite the poor history, then go ahead. The good part about going back and looking at previous ROI projections is that it will tell you the forecast accuracy of those projections. If the estimated ROIs were accurate plus or minus 15 percent of the actual ROI, then you can safely assume that the new ROIs produced by the same individuals and organizations will be in that range and of good quality. However, before reaching any conclusions, you will always want to ask: "Are there any new factors or considerations in the current analysis that didn't exist in the prior analysis?"

If the organization's ROI estimates were plus or minus 25 percent or more of the actual ROI, then make the use of ROI conditional.

I am sure that no one at your company or organization tweaks or massages their ROI numbers to "bump them up" a little or a lot with hopes of getting a project or initiative selected, but it does happen in other companies. If your organization never goes back to critique ROI estimates and then hold the estimator accountable for those estimates, expect a lot of massaging of ROI data by those trying to increase the odds of their project gaining approval. The program manager has to assure that the project selection process uses valid data and/or understands the deficiency the data has in it.

TIP

When this discussion comes up in my training of program managers, most of them say that their organization never looks back at previous estimates. Invariably a program manager will make the comment that "Circumstances have changed. There is no point in going back because the circumstances are different now." This is not a valid excuse for not going back and analyzing. It is simply another reason not to give too much credence to the use of ROI and financial measures.

In today's high-technology environment it is difficult to project what technology will be available three years from now and almost impossible to nail it down five years from now. Even so, your decisions are only as good as your ability to forecast, and your ability to forecast is documented by your forecast history. That's why you need to continually track it. If you are factoring ROI as an important decision criterion, you must look at and maintain performance history.

Strategic Elements of the Portfolio

The chicken and egg question in portfolio management is: "Does the amount of capital investment available dictate strategy, or does your strategy dictate the amount of capital investment?" From a developmental perspective, purists would say that when identifying strategy or strategic alternatives you should not restrict or inhibit your thinking. The sky's the limit. No boundaries. This process of developing strategies with no boundaries is valid, but the resulting strategies will have to be matched with the budget. The strategy may be so good that you'll want to seek out alternative funding; however, in the absence of alternative funding, someone has to take the Blue Sky to the meat and potatoes the organization can implement within existing constraints. This means difficult choices.

From a psychological point of view, one of the hardest things to do is abandon a previous course of action, especially if the course of action was successful before and the performance or potential is now sliding. Our innate desire to cling to what we know and are comfortable with is exactly why existing initiatives should come under more scrutiny. Some organizations even set targets or establish percentages for what has to be spent on new or out-of-the-box initiatives because they want to make sure the organization is looking ahead at new and different opportunities or ways of doing business. Setting aside a percentage of the portfolio for this is a good strategy.

Realize that "set-asides" are nothing but target percentages or resource levels for certain aspects of the portfolio. A portfolio analysis or sanity check will show the portfolio allocations across a number of perspectives. A sanity check involves answering questions like

- How are our projects allocated in terms of dollar value and number of projects?
  - Small projects to large projects?
  - Maintenance projects to new development projects?
  - Across the organization?
  - Geographically?
  - Across the supplier base?

- ○ Across technologies?
- ○ Across the customer base?
- ○ High risk to low risk?

Looking at the funded projects or proposed project allocations from multiple perspectives tells a story and may cause reallocation of resources or reprioritization of projects if the perspective is inconsistent with strategic goals or is judged to be too risky. These perspectives can provide the basis for guidelines like "No more than 50 percent of our projects should be high risk." The program manager has to look at the portfolio from the strategic level to ensure balance of risk, opportunity, and effectiveness.

A common set-aside opportunity for large programs is for small projects because it may be difficult for small projects that make sense to go through the approval cycle that exists in some large programs. These small projects often have a difficult time competing with projects that are 10, 100, or 10,000 times its value. Such a challenge is common in large organizations that manage multimillion and multibillion dollar initiatives.

SCENARIO

How does the organization identify and fund small, commonsense projects that often lie beneath the threshold for new funding consideration, but that exceed and/or are out of scope of the sponsoring organizations operational budget? I was once involved in an initiative at NASA that created a sublevel board with its own budget to solicit, identify, and approve projects that ordinarily did not warrant high-level attention because they were not major program issues. This initiative was extremely successful and had the additional benefit of increasing morale because personnel at lower levels now had a rapid way to submit an idea that could be quickly approved. Small projects often positively impact morale because they provide more opportunities for people to finish something and that creates personnel satisfaction.

All organizations need to have a method that allows smart things to be executed quickly, even if they are small smart things. Setting aside a portion of the portfolio for this works very well. Figure 9-2 is from the book *Augustine's Laws* by Norm R. Augustine. It shows the likelihood of a good idea making its way through the system depending upon the number of layers of management that exist and approvals that are required. The probability of successfully accomplishing any objective declines in a very calculable manner as the number of layers in the approval process increases. Please note that the real and devastating effect of a slow or bureaucratic approval process is that people stop submitting ideas and then stop thinking.

Good portfolio management includes accounting for regulatory or mandated projects and expenditures separately. It is also

FIGURE 9.2 Idea Survivability

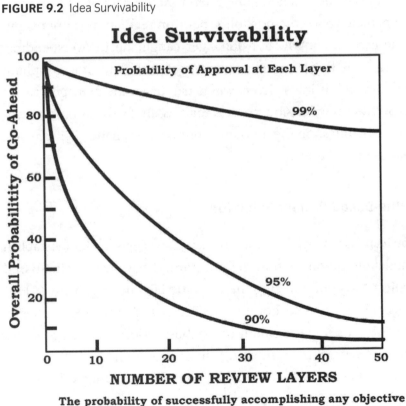

The probability of successfully accomplishing any objective declines in a very calculative manner as the number of layers in the approval process increases.

Source: Norman R. Augustine, *Augustine's Law*, 6th edition, American Institute of Aeronautics and Astronautics, 1997.

important to keep a history of the percentage of the portfolio dollars that are spent on regulated activities. In today's U.S. business environment, compliance to the regulatory "flavors of the day" is becoming a greater expense and challenge.

There is a line where adequate profitability ceases to exist given the amount of regulation imposed at the state and federal level. As a result of this, companies are moving out of certain states to other states or moving out of the United States completely through a variety of means. Also, some publicly traded companies are going private to reduce the expense of complying with government regulation. Therefore, managing and tracking the percentage of the portfolio spent on regulation is important. Take care to comply, but don't get caught up in overspending. The goal is to be compliant and profitable and not compliant and out of business. Even when the program manager is not involved in the decision process for this, he or she should understand and question the amount spent on compliance if it impacts the program budget.

Value-Based Project Selection

You can use many methods to select projects and/or establish budget allocations within the program. I have used Value-Based Project Selection utilizing the Analytic Hierarchy Process (AHP) with great success for both private sector and government clients. The AHP uses matrix math to establish priorities among values and alternatives by comparing them head-to-head. This can be done in Microsoft Excel, but the use of preexisting software to implement AHP makes the task easy.

The beauty of the Analytic Hierarchy Process is that it is simple, mathematically sound, and establishes buy-in among stakeholders. You can use it in its pure form or you can use it to create scoring sheets and templates. The power in the AHP process is how it defines the value structure for decision making and can include any relevant qualitative measures such as company reputation. It goes beyond ROI and other financial measures by requiring the definition of all the values necessary for the decision.

A lot of organizations think they have such definitions, but AHP requires these structures to be weighted by the decision makers with head-to-head comparisons to produce a weighted priority for each value. This drives accountability to decision makers, because they can't say "everything is important." Some values are more important than others.

My experience has been that these head-to-head comparisons result in a new level of understanding of organizational values among stakeholders, which is why high degrees of "buy-in" occur when this method is properly applied. Realize that AHP, or any other tool that discriminates among projects, is just a subset of the portfolio management process. A project's AHP score could be a part of the business case or used to discriminate among projects after business cases have been developed. But AHP has the distinct advantage, because it can factor in attributes beyond the financial that are difficult to quantify, and that is paramount in today's rapidly changing and complex technological environment.

"Buy-in" is a critical goal in the portfolio management process. Since every initiative will not be able to be funded, all stakeholders will not get what they want. Therefore, when considering the effectiveness of a portfolio management structure, a key element is the degree to which the method produces buy-in among the stakeholders. After all, there is little benefit in having a process that selects the right projects if the stakeholders involved will sometimes use various tactics to fight the project during the implementation phase. That is why the program manager must work with program stakeholders to establish realistic expectations. Lack of resources and the inability of the organization to implement the proposed change can contribute to unrealistic expectations. The program manager has to partner with the stakeholders to resolve or pacify issues when there are differing expectations.

KEYSTONES

Portfolio Management Essentials

1. A tool can provide a recommended list of projects, but this is just input to the decision maker's judgment; his or her judgment should prevail.
2. Organizations that regulate input to ensure that capacity is controlled and that the system utilization rarely exceeds 90 percent actually accomplish more over a year's timeframe than organizations that don't regulate input.
3. A sure sign of a lack of leadership is the statement "everything is top priority."
4. Sound portfolio management involves assessing where your program has been, understanding where your program is today, and driving where your program is going.
5. Measuring the effectiveness of projects after delivery causes customers and stakeholders to carefully consider projects before proposing them.
6. The sooner you identify and acknowledge project failure the greater the cost savings.
7. Three essential questions every proposed project should answer are: Why do this at all? Why do it this way? Why do it now?
8. No customer or stakeholder should be allowed to change or fix anything he or she doesn't understand.
9. Return on Investment (ROI) is fraught with pitfalls and is the most over-rated project selection method.
10. All organizations need to have a method that allows smart things to be executed quickly, even if they are small smart things.

Positive Program Outcomes

Ultimately, program managers are judged on results. Creating the positive program culture that facilitates excellent project management should correspondingly produce excellent results. Having the correct program manager attributes, knowing how to manage stakeholders, implementing the most effective program process strategy, deploying good execution processes, building strong program teams, planning well-organized program communication processes, ensuring thorough risk management, and linking the program to organizational strategy are pathways to program clarity and corresponding success.

Framing Success

Very often the program manager feels squeezed between the company's goal of making a profit and maintaining high levels of customer satisfaction. That's why the program manager must "frame success," in terms both of the manager's work with customers and of his or her leadership within the organization. Make no mistake . . . this framing is critical.

I know a program manager whose leadership team gave him two not-so-subtle hints about his relationship with the customer. The first hint was a cartoon picture of a dead man in a coffin. The caption read: "Here lies the program manager that gave the customers everything they wanted!" The second hint was a job application for the Salvation Army, since he obviously wanted to unselfishly serve the needy without adequate payment.

The following framing tips apply to newly assigned program managers, but are also applicable to all programs if adequate framing of success criteria has not already been accomplished.

- A recently assigned program manager should spend his or her first weeks doing a full assessment of the scope of work under the program's control. A common fault of "newly assigned" program managers is jumping to conclusions based on limited information or information provided by a select few people. Information is coming at a rapid pace and you must assess the entire picture to ensure good decisions.
- Expect to be bombarded with a variety of problems and issues. You must assess and prioritize each in light of program goals.
- Program personnel will also have expectations of you, and those expectations must also be framed for success. If not,

the program personnel will be disappointed with anything less than superhero results.

- Start framing the process by:
  - Performing a gap analysis on all program performance aspects.
  - Determining what you can realistically accomplish based on the resources you have available. Obviously, if you have performed a thorough gap analysis there will be items that you will have to table or set aside for future action. Put these in priority order with the resource costs and obstacles associated with them defined.
  - Defining how you and then your boss will measure your success.
  - Shaping the lens through which people (your boss, stakeholders, and program personnel) define success.

Calculated Failure

Like many program management functions, "lens shaping" doesn't occur instantaneously. Therefore, you need to exploit every opportunity to reinforce or shape the lens. Toward that end, calculated failure can be a critical element for driving organizational change and/or lens shaping.

Although program and project managers are often shocked when I instruct them to do this in training classes, nevertheless every system should have calculated failure points. Calculated failure is controllable. For example, in an electrical system fuses serve as calculated failure points. The fuse protects the system and is the trigger point for system evaluation to assess the cause of the failure. If you don't make calculated decisions about failure points, then failure is subject to happen haphazardly or in unanticipated areas.

I once had a client at a Fortune 100 company whose program was overworked and she wanted to prioritize all of her projects. Her employees were working sixty-plus hours per week with no relief in sight. When she presented her plan to her leadership team, they told her there was no need to prioritize the work because her organization had not missed any deadlines. That is, she had never blown a fuse, which was what I advised her to start doing (calculated failure). As the program manager she is responsible for the long-term viability of the program, not just the short-term deadlines. At the pace she was working her group it was only a matter of time before one of her key program personnel would quit or get sick, resulting in an uncalculated failure with significant repercussions beyond her control.

Organizations typically overwork personnel in response to internal and external demands. When relief does not come through logic, negotiation, and/or persuasion, and a fuse blows, you need to exploit and leverage this event for change. Address the failure, assess the organizational ramifications for the cause, and use these ramifications to take the organization in a direction of positive change.

Creating Positive Customer Satisfaction

Nothing creates customer satisfaction like doing a good job. Just as good meat makes its own gravy, doing a good job creates goodwill and trust among all participants. So while framing success is important, managing the customer's "perception" of the process and deliverables is equally important. So a good job, good framing, and managing the customer's perception are all elements of customer satisfaction.

For example, suppose I have a major event to celebrate with my wife. I choose to take her to one of those ultrafancy restaurants. You know, the ones, where they make you wait even though the restaurant may not be full and they use that silver tool to scrape the crumbs off the fancy tablecloth between courses. These restaurants don't let you even peek into the kitchen. If they did, you might find out they dropped your wife's baked potato on the floor, and because of the "five second" rule, they just put the potato back on the plate before they served it to her. Or maybe those little trees they stick in food at the fancy restaurant were actually stored in a grungy bin on the floor. Perhaps the skillets they created all of those fancy sauces in were so dirty you wouldn't use them at home. The bottom line is that your level of customer satisfaction would be significantly diminished if you were able to see the fancy meal come together. Presentation of the meal is part of perception and impacts the overall satisfaction with the meal.

Despite all of the benefits of "partnering" and "concurrent engineering" from a customer-satisfaction perspective, you need to isolate the customer as much as possible from the "messiness" of creating the deliverable. This is not always possible, but the program manager needs to understand and communicate to project managers and program staff that the customer does not need to know everything. The program manager should also make sure that project managers have control over who on their project teams has permission to talk to the customer. The boundaries limiting what program personnel can say to, or what subjects can be broached with the customer should also be defined. Customer satisfaction with the deliverable has been torpedoed many times by technical personnel who dwell on the negative aspects of the deliverable, even when those negatives are grossly outweighed by positive aspects. Perception plays an important role in customer satisfaction and must be managed. Figure 10.1 shows the typical baseline for a project.

As this figure illustrates, the plan is smooth, but the actual implementation is filled with ups and downs and adjustments. Therefore, create with the customer an agreeable threshold for

FIGURE 10.1 Typical Baseline Plan for a Project

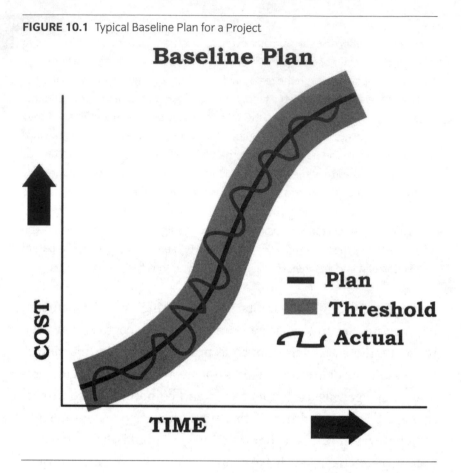

Baseline Plan

when you will communicate things that are beyond normal status. In other words, the customer is not contacted until the threshold is violated or you are sure you are going to violate it. This buffers the customer from the constant noise that exists with implementation and increases customer satisfaction. In fact, the program manager can have the same type of agreement with project managers about their projects, establishing thresholds for when they must come to the program manager for guidance with a problem or issue. This serves to eliminate a lot of unnecessary communication or fuss about items unworthy of discussion and ensures that project managers seek program manager guidance when in trouble.

I worked my way through college at a furniture warehouse owned by furniture mogul John F. Lawhon. Lawhon would sometimes sell a seven-piece living room set at extremely cheap prices, namely because the quality of that particular set was equally cheap. In fact, in some cases the furniture was so cheap that a single warehouseman could carry a sofa and love seat by himself. Sometimes we would even play catch with the furniture in the back. But in front of the customer we were instructed to carry the furniture as if it were heavy by using two people when only one was necessary. I also noticed that one warehouseman consistently got more tips than anyone else. I asked him how he did it and he stated that he always told the customer about the "extra" things he did to "protect" their investment, and that the way he loaded the furniture made it easier for them to unload it safely when they got home. He really did nothing more than any other warehousemen except relay this information to the customer. When I started telling the customer what I was doing to protect their investment, my tips quadrupled.

Maximizing customer satisfaction with perception control is not about keeping the customer in the dark, but about communicating the things that make the customer feel good about the product or service. Ingrain this concept into your project managers. As a customer, I don't want to see how my fast food was prepared, but I do want to enjoy it. I know these are simple examples for what is most likely a complex product or service your program is providing, but human nature is fundamentally the same regardless of the scope of the deliverable. So while the customer may insist on seeing how the sausage is made, don't expect them to enjoy it as much when they know how it's processed. Your job is to distract them so that they don't see the gory parts unless it is absolutely necessary for the success of the deliverable.

I have a friend who enjoys a salad from a particular restaurant famous for their salads. There is nothing magical about salads, and she had tried at home several times to make the same salad the restaurant serves, but it wasn't quite the same. So she spoke to several waiters at the restaurant about this, and finally one told her the secret: Just before the salad is served, they sprinkle powdered sugar all over it. The sugar is so fine that it dissolves instantly and customers don't know it's there, but they know that the salad tastes good.

What are the "powdered sugar" equivalents you can provide for your customer that make your level of service special? This is something worthy of brainstorming with your program team. One company I know takes the entire team and the customer to dinner to celebrate every milestone. Your powdered sugar equivalent doesn't have to be that large or expensive. In fact, never underestimate the power of the quality trinket (T-shirts, pens, day planners, birthday gifts, etc.). The project could have a $10 million deliverable, but it's often the small gifts that take customer satisfaction over the top. You need to budget for your "powdered sugar" equivalents and/or leverage the marketing budget for them. If this money is not approved, it becomes a necessary out-of-pocket expense for the program manager.

Tech-Expert-itis

Organizations have a tendency to promote individuals to project manager who have demonstrated technical expertise. There is nothing wrong with this when these technical experts have been prepared, trained, and/or mentored to accept the project management role. Unfortunately, a lot of organizations don't provide this preparation and then suffer the unfortunate consequences of tech-expert-itis, a debilitating condition that causes people to believe that technical expertise in one area equals expertise or proficiency in other areas. These tech people tend to apply the solution or methods they know to all other areas with varying degrees of success and failure. The dangerous part of tech-expert-itis is that the diseased tech expert blames others when things don't work. This is also a recipe for poor customer satisfaction.

During a recent hurricane season, I had to get a new roof twice in one month. Because of that, the roofer and I became very good friends. The roofer told me that he had gotten a new air-conditioning unit a few years ago and was concerned that it would be exposed to all the torrential rains we receive in Florida. Since he was a roofer, he built a miniroof to cover his air-conditioning unit. He also thought the shade would help keep his cooling costs lower. Well, that air-conditioning unit that should have lasted at least ten years failed after only three years. His friend in the air-conditioning business came by and inspected his unit and told him that the roof he built caused the premature failure. It turns out that his air-conditioning unit was designed to be rained on, because rain is part of the process the air-conditioning unit uses to clean the coils. It's another classic case of tech-expert-itis, this time on the part of my roofer!

To avoid tech-expert-itis, the program manager has to always examine solutions proposed by project managers and technical experts in order to be on the lookout for biases against alternate solutions. This includes biases against the simple solution. Here is a good example of what I mean: One year while I was working there, NASA had a space shuttle on the launch pad that had developed a problem with an electronics box. Every electronics box in the space shuttle has a small army of technical experts who manage every aspect of it. The problem this box was having was going to force a rollback from the launch pad, creating a lengthy schedule delay and high costs to NASA. After significant deliberation about sophisticated means and tests to evaluate the box, a junior level project engineer (not even a part of the army of technical experts assigned to the box) proposed using Ohm's Law (voltage equals current times resistance) to test the box. Ohm's Law is the simplest formula an electrical engineer can use. The junior engineer was right and the use of something as simple as Ohm's Law, which had been overlooked by the technical experts prevented a rollback of the space shuttle and allowed the launch to proceed as scheduled.

So beware. Furthermore, tech-expert-itis also causes people to think of complicated solutions where simple solutions exist. That's why the program manager needs to coach project managers in looking for the simple solution when dealing with technical gurus. A simple solution does not exist in every circumstance, but you should always be on the hunt for it.

Lessons Learned

Many organizations repeat the same project management mistakes over and over. It is human nature to want to forget failure and bury the memory. But we must learn from our mistakes or we are destined to repeat them. When an organization continually repeats the same types of mistakes that result in failure, then it is usually not a project manager problem. Recurring problems are often a symptom of things beyond the project manager's control.

To keep recurring problems at a minimum, many organizations create a "lessons learned" database. Often these databases are not effective tools. In my training class I ask participants if their company has a lessons-learned database. I follow this up by asking, "Who has looked at it in the past six months?" Nine times out of ten, no one raises their hand. That's because most project managers don't have time and/or won't take the time to look at the lessons-learned database. So, storing lessons learned is one thing. Ensuring that the organization actually learns from the failure is something else. This is where the challenge lies, and the program manager has to ensure that the organization is learning from the mistakes of the past.

Like every parent, I possess a lot of wisdom and life lessons that I would like to pass on to my teenage sons. Some things they accept, and some they don't, due to immaturity or their natural teenager arrogance. Immaturity and arrogance are also what the organization has to fight in order to take lessons learned out of the abstract and move them into the concrete realm of achievable improvements in performance.

If your company has a lessons-learned database, pull something from it periodically to review with project managers. You can also maintain your own top-ten list of most valuable painful personal lessons learned and share it with every new program stakeholder, project manager, or support personnel. This also provides the program or project manager the opportunity to ask others what lessons learned they can apply to the program. Please note that lessons-learned database is not just about mistakes, but should also include documenting situations that worked and opportunities that were exploited. If your company has a lessons learned database, you need to examine its access statistics, as these will tell you the usefulness of the database. If it is not being used effectively, then it needs to be formally assessed.

Institutionalize Plagiarism

It is important for the program manager to create an environment of plagiarism. I don't mean plagiarism in the usual sense (of stealing someone else's words or ideas), but plagiarism in the sense of mature and disciplined organizations copying and institutionalizing what has proven to be effective. The program manager must do this on a personal and organizational level.

TIP

There was a television program, years ago, that highlighted a company that gave an annual award for the best copied idea. There is nothing wrong with creativity, but human beings have been on the planet a long time. Make use of all that prior creativity and knowledge.

SCENARIO

Early in my NASA career, there was an incident that damaged a multimillion-dollar piece of space shuttle flight hardware. The investigative report about the incident was professionally done, a first-class job, and I filed it away. Many years later, there was another incident in the Space Program in which a million-dollar piece of hardware was damaged, and I was one of three people charged with investigating the incident. We had a very short deadline in which to complete the investigation. I showed the team the previous report, and we used it as a guide for our process and report. As a result, we received numerous compliments on the professionalism and quality of our product.

Over the course of your career you will do many different tasks. Whenever you come across something that screams "quality" and "excellent" work, be sure to keep it. This also applies to people. As a program manager you should keep up with high-quality people. Whenever you come across them, within or outside your company, get their contact information and stay in touch with them. On an organizational level, tell your project managers to always be on the lookout for best practices they can copy from suppliers, customers, or other stakeholders.

Also remember that people behave according to how they are rewarded. I was once conducting a training session for a leading telecommunications company that values engineering and rewards patents. As I walked down the hallway of this company, I saw patent after patent after patent on the wall, and that was just for the patents awarded in the past year! I was impressed. Someone in my class saw me looking at all the patents and I told her how impressive this was. She told me not to be impressed because from her perspective the wall of patents was part of the company's problem. She stated, "Because my company places so much emphasis and rewards on patents, engineers make things more complex than necessary just to get a patent. When we take our competitor's product apart and compare it with the same product we make, our product has two and a half times the component parts for the same functionality as the competitor's product. Two and a half times the number of parts! This means more material to buy, more time to assemble, more spare parts to maintain, more opportunities for failure. The mind-set of complexity is killing us, but I am not an engineer and they don't listen to me."

Be very careful what you reward. Look for unintended consequences of the **TIP** reward and adjust accordingly. Rewarding simplicity and copying good ideas takes the program in a positive direction.

Slow, Steady, Gentle Pressure

The program manager has to find ways to drive results from project managers and ensure that project managers know how to get results from project team members. Putting people under pressure works. Pressure is a good thing and should be a well-used tool in the program manager's tool kit. Pressure works whether you are managing up or down. However, I do not believe in deploying tremendous pressure, because the subsequent stress levels can harm people and relationships. Tremendous pressure can, in the right circumstances, for a brief period of time and using strict controls be very effective in achieving positive outcomes.

Over my career I have seen two program managers very successfully deliver program goals by using tremendous pressure. In both cases, while all the tasks got completed, there was "blood in the streets" during the process. Both of these leaders felt passionately about the importance of the deliverables, to the degree that when people in the organization quit, got sick, or broke down, it didn't matter to them and the pace and pressure never relented; the deliverable was that important.

One of these leaders' programs provided public housing for the poor. The organization had been suffering from ineptness prior to his taking over, and since he took over with his direct, high-pressure style, there is no question that thousands of poor people are much better off because of him and his management style, and they will be better off for many years to come. Today, his organization is widely recognized for being efficiently run. However, the turnover rate of personnel in his organization is very high, due to the pressure he puts on people. But from his perspective, the high turnover is a natural outcome of his high-pressure style, and he works around it. His style is not my style, and I wouldn't recommend it. Programs and people are usually ruined when tremendous pressure is consistently deployed and the success of these two individuals was unusual and yet it provoked negative ramifications for program personnel although program objectives were achieved.

I recommend slow, steady, and gentle pressure. With this kind of pressure, even though you are putting people in a stressful situation, you are doing so judiciously and know when to let up. I believe that the program manager has to apply pressure, but you must also ensure that it is not too much pressure. Whenever you encounter nonperformance, you must assess the human side of the issue. Is there a health or personal reason for the nonperformance? People get sick and have personal tragedies that can transcend the importance of the milestone, so you are obligated to look out for program goals and your personnel's well-being to a degree. This is in the long-term best interest of the program.

There are many ways for you to generate this kind of slow, steady, and gentle pressure to drive work to get done. Publicly displaying a list of late deliverables, delayed decisions, and troubled projects is one way. This should be done consistently, not just when there is one thing you want to highlight. Tying deliverables or milestone achievements to bonuses or tangible performance ratings is another. Praise can be one of the most powerful ways to put pressure on people. Learn to positively set high expectations for people so that they will be uncomfortable if they don't meet your expectations. The client who puts me under the most pressure publicly praises me in front of new stakeholders for past successes and my having exceeded expectations in all of our past engagements. He effectively uses praise to set a very high bar, which puts me under pressure to achieve, and this brings out my best work.

Program Performance Analysis

The program manager should always monitor and judge program performance over time. Performance against business goals should be automatic. Therefore, the program performance analysis described here is not against business goals. Why? Because you can properly execute and have unfortunate circumstances that do not allow the program to achieve the current business goals. Conversely, business goals can be met when program execution is poor if the market or business environment is kind enough to you.

As a program manager, you need to judge execution so that it can be continually improved, as improved execution makes achievement of business goals much more likely over the long term. And often, positive business growth has a way of masking poorly run programs. Therefore, program performance analysis is best done with metrics, and metric data is much more valuable when there is a history or something with which to contrast the current data. Metrics the program manager should consider include the following:

1. Feedback from the customer. Having standard processes for obtaining customer feedback can provide valuable information and help identify or prioritize systemic problems throughout the organization.

2. Compliance with process. Having processes is good. The next step is measuring compliance with those processes, as the level of compliance tracked over time tells a story. Examine the root cause of noncompliance issues as well as trends to identify problems or opportunities.

3. Requirements alignment (planned and delivered). The program manager can measure how well the requirements of the projects being implemented match up with the organization's objectives. This sounds very basic, but frequently there are significant gaps between these two. Both planned and delivered requirements may need to be checked, as some projects may provide deliverables that are significantly different than what was planned. Checking these things is just another way of instilling organizational discipline.

4. Stakeholder stability. How often program stakeholders change or change their perspective is a measure of program stability. This case refers to the high-level stakeholders and key vendors and suppliers that the program is dependent on.

5. Project manager stability. How long the program maintains its project managers and other key personnel is also a measure of program stability. Tracking this data over time can help the program manager bolster his or her position when program personnel are being raided.

6. Calendar stability. Does your calendar remain stable for the morning, for the day, for the week? An unstable program manager's calendar rolls downhill. It is difficult for project managers to maintain stable calendars when their leaders' calendars are always changing. If the project manager's calendar is always changing, then so is the project team's. The stability of the calendars of the program manager and the project manager are a reflection of program health.

7. Program schedule stability. The stability of the program schedule *over time* is a good measure of program health. You are looking for inconsistent patterns in the stability of your schedule and the root cause for those patterns.

8. Improvement initiative history. The program management role requires continual tracking of the program's success over time. Program managers and the organization often take for granted the progress that has been made over time, and tracking it is not only motivational, but also makes it easier to sell other improvements and can quell unwarranted criticism of the program.

The measurements mentioned are suggestions. All will add some degree of value, depending upon your program's level of maturity and environment. But don't get carried away and measure too many things. Whatever you measure, make sure you collect data frequently enough to calculate natural process variation. That is, do not overreact to "perceived" bad numbers. Always make sure you clearly understand the story behind the number before creating a fix or plan of attack.

Additionally, always establish goals, and do not be afraid to evaluate and change metrics as the process matures. Use metrics as a tool to garner control of stakeholders and customers when possible.

SCENARIO

An IT organization started tracking the percentage of projects they were working in situations where the customers had not signed off on the requirements, as well as the percentage of projects being worked for which the customers did not have their business process mapped. Posting these metrics was not only "eye-opening" for some stakeholders, but it also drove their customers in a direction of positive improvement.

Invest some time and think strategically about metrics, what problems they can expose, and how they can exert pressure to drive the organization in a positive direction. Begin with the end in mind. Think about the decisions the metric will allow you to make. Only then will you develop good and usable metrics.

Closing Thoughts

Presence, relationship building, consistency, effective questioning, decision making, and mentoring are the program management leadership traits described in Chapter 2. The program manager also needs doggedness. Since programs are continual in nature, the program manager must persevere in good times and bad, all the while remaining focused on program objectives, improving the program's ability to execute, and increasing the capability of program personnel.

At the program level, many of the problems you are trying to fix are entrenched in culture, process, and tradition. These problems are not easily or instantaneously fixed; rather, you must continually hammer them over a period of time before a breakthrough can be achieved. The following quote from noted American journalist Jacob Riis applies to the program manager.

> When nothing seems to help, I go look at a stonecutter hammering away at his rock, perhaps a hundred times without as much as a crack showing in it. Yet at the hundred and first blow it will split in two, and I know it was not that blow that did it, but all that had gone before.

Creating positive culture change involves relentless hammering away by the program manager, who must have the doggedness to get used to deferred gratification. The resulting positive changes often reveal themselves later when previous actions that helped facilitate the changes are forgotten.

Program Outcome

1. Very often the program manager feels squeezed between the company's goal of making a profit and maintaining high levels of customer satisfaction.
2. Calculated failure can be a critical element for driving organizational change and/or lens shaping.
3. Nothing creates customer satisfaction like doing a good job.
4. You need to isolate the customer as much as possible from the "messiness" of creating the deliverable.
5. Maximizing customer satisfaction with perception control is not about keeping the customer in the dark, but about communicating the things that make the customer feel good about the product or service.
6. Tech-expert-itis can be a problem when people falsely believe that technical expertise in one area equals expertise or proficiency in other areas.
7. The program manager has to always examine proposed solutions from project managers and technical experts to check for biases that exclude alternate solutions.
8. Lessons learned are not just about mistakes, but also include documenting things that worked and opportunities that were exploited.
9. Be very careful what you reward. Look for unintended consequences of the rewards and adjust accordingly.
10. Program performance analysis goes beyond achieving business goals and cost targets, and is best done with program metrics.

Glossary

Agile project management—A methodology to create iterative and incremental deliveries while being adaptive.

Analytic Hierarchy Process (AHP)—A decision process that establishes a hierarchical weighting criteria through pair-wise comparisons and evaluates alternatives against each other relative to the weighting criteria.

Business case measures—Metrics like Return on Investment (ROI) or Net Present Value (NPV) used to help evaluate and prioritize business cases for potential projects.

Buy-in—Agreement and commitment among the team and/or stakeholders on a set of circumstances or plan of action.

Change control board (CCB)—A group or individual acting as a board to approve all program or project changes.

Change management process—A process that controls program or project changes and provides traceability and accountability for all changes.

Chaotic project management culture—A culture that renders the project manager ineffective due to instability of leadership, processes, resources, requirements, and shifting or nonexistent priorities.

Company culture—The collection of processes, attitudes, beliefs, and values that characterize a company.

Earned value—A management tool that characterize project progress through object measures based on actual costs, planned cost and work completed to date.

Effective questioning—Utilizing a feel for the organization in a manner that results in questions that expose the root cause of issues, challenges or opportunities.

ERP System—A system that integrates all processes and data for an organization into one overarching structure.

Feedback process—A structure that requests the input of stakeholders and team members to improve performance of an individual, team, or organization.

5 × 5 risk matrix—A qualitative risk management tool that plots probability and impact for risks, allowing them to be consistently assessed by an organization.

Global environments—A variety of business, cultural, process, and government surroundings that must be addressed by companies with worldwide operations.

Kurzweil's Law—A principle that characterizes the growth of technology as exponential, described in the essay "The Law of Accelerating Returns."

Operations management—The management of business processes and resources for the continual production of goods and/or services.

Organizational culture—The collection of processes, attitudes, beliefs, and values that characterize an organization

Organizational discipline—Compliance by an organization to its processes, rules, and structure.

Planning horizon—The timeframe for the amount of work you can reasonably schedule based on project requirements and availability of resources.

Program culture—The collection of processes, attitudes, beliefs, and values that characterize a program.

Program environment—A collection of projects and/or operations that may or may not be a stand-alone organization

Program management office (PMO)—A group that establishes and manages project management policies and in some organizational implementations may also manage projects.

Program manager role—Assuring that business and program targets are met through the leadership of project managers and the establishment of a culture conducive to successful project implementations.

Program performance analysis—Evaluation of metric data that allows the assessment of program execution effectiveness.

Project culture—The collection of processes, attitudes, beliefs, and values that characterize a project.

Project manager role—Assuring successful project delivery through management of the project's cost, schedule, and scope attributes.

Project phase—The categorization of a project's status (design phase, build phase, etc.), usually consistent with the organization's project management methodology.

Project portfolio management—Assuring the program is working on the set of projects that provides the most value to the organization without exceeding resource requirements.

Project status process—The process leaders use to assess the current health and challenges of projects and to emphasize issues that need management attention.

Relationship capital—The amount of influence a program manager can wield through the organization by establishing relationships of ever-increasing trust, internal and external to the organization.

Risk response matrix—A risk management tool that looks at the integrated relationships between risk response options so that the best overall response for a project or program is chosen.

Self-regulation—The organization acts and performs just as the program manager would want it to, even if the program manager is not present.

Spiral development cycles—A methodology that integrates design and prototyping in stages with incremental deliveries.

Stage gate—A checkpoint in the project management process that usually requires verification of project deliverables and process integrity prior to proceeding to the next phase of the project.

Stakeholders—Anyone or anything impacted upon by a project or program, with customers and organizational leadership frequently being the most important stakeholders.

Structured methodology—A defined methodology outlining project management processes usually detailed by project phase.

Value-based project selection—Selecting projects based on their value to an organization, usually including nonfinancial criteria as part of the value structure.

Index

The Handbook of Program Management